T0137572

It's A Part of Life

ONAWA K. PLEASURES

It's A Part of Life

It's Life

Author
Onawa K. Pleasures

It's a Part of Life

ONAWA K. PLEASURES

Order this book online at www.trafford.com
or email orders@trafford.com

Most Trafford titles are also available at major online book retailers.

Printed in the United States of America.

ISBN: 978-1-4269-3806-1 (sc)
ISBN: 978-1-4269-6531-9 (e)

Library of Congress Control Number: 2011904674

Trafford rev. 04/06/2011

www.trafford.com

North America & International
toll-free: 1 888 232 4444 (USA & Canada)
phone: 250 383 6864 ♦ fax: 812 355 4082

Acknowledgements

*Kenneth Bynums someone that
believed in me and my words*

Credits to the following;

*Graphic Artist
Trafford Graphics Department*

*Financer
Kenneth Bynums*

Introduction

This story setting takes place during the
late mid-1960's through 1999. With music of the
time helping set the mood while three siblings coming
of age during time of social changes and living the ups
and
downs of their lives and growing as people. Learning
about
fun, love, responsibility, troubled times and even death.

Marie..............

It's early June and a bit of a nip in the air tonight as I'm serenaded by the music coming from my brother Junie's' bedroom - Marvin Gaye, the Four Tops, the Temptations, and the Supremes just to name a few, I'm reading the most recent letter I've received from Mike. Although there's a nip in the air, what I'm reading is making me feel quite warm. You know? I never intended on such a simple little correspondence to some lonely soldier to go so far. Mike is saying that he'll be returning to the states soon, and is looking forward to seeing me in person. We've only seen each other by the photos we've exchanged. Okay, okay there's been quite a few pictures and some of course, a little sensual and sexy. I do have to say, people say I'm attractive. (smile)

Ring.... Ring...it's the telephone."Hello, just reading a letter from Mike. Oh yeah, who's going? Let me find something to wear, be ready in an hour, alright an hour and a half", I said to my girlfriend Dasia. Dasia said, "Look, we'll pick you up, my brother and his friends don't know about us meeting them there, but girl, his friend is fine. So I figured just by chance we'd run into them at the bar. Get it?" Sighing, "Dasia, I got it, let me go so I can get ready. See you in a few. I have to lay here another two or three minutes to finish my daydream", I told her.

Opening my closet door, my closet is huge, not that it's full of clothes, but I have some funky going out outfits. Let's see what should I put on? I thought, how about this mini skirt and that lime green halter. No no no, maybe this instead, my jean mini skirt, with the white top, go-go boots, my bikini panties, and pantyhose. My bosom are very perky so I need no bra and the material is just thin enough to show a slight imprint of my nipples, but nowhere near being brazen. I laid it on my bed then went to shower, apply my new Mabeline make-up, with this head full of hair is too much to do in such short notice so I put on my new flip hair piece, (a faux). Walking back to my bed I can hear Mom and Aunt Kate downstairs talking about some of everything and everybody. Mom and Aunt Kate are sisters, very very close sisters, people usually think they're twins.

Actually, my Grand parents and all their children live within about seven blocks, even some of my father's sisters and brothers live within the same seven or eight block radius, so most of the time you'll see us together. Not all of us at once, of course but, some cousins, sisters, brothers, grandparents with their children or grands, in-laws or some combination of family.

It was only mandatory for me to let my brothers, Junie the eldest just back from the Air Force, and Allen, just registered with the Air Force, know I'm leaving and where I'll be. Allen had appointed himself as my guardian, whether I want him to be or not Listen, I had my own way of taking care of them also. I did have to admit both of my brothers are tall, talented, fine and a lot of fun. So I had to guard them from the ladies also, you know what I mean?

I had gotten dressed and went downstairs to wait for my ride.
"Hi Aunt Kate", we kissed on the cheek. Then I sat down at the kitchen table to join the conversation until my ride arrived. Both my Mom and her sister were easy on the eye. Average height, hair always looking nice, skin the color of medium light toast, Aunt Kate's hazel eyes were tinted gray, Doris my mother, her hazel eyes were tinted green. "Doris" Aunt Kate said, "you know Sarah just don't care. She's always thought she was cute, but Reanie gave her what she wanted."

Doris looked up from putting her S&S stamps into the book, "I know Reanie whipped her ass", said Doris.

We had to laugh, see Reanie is our cousin. Her mother is my Grandfather's sister. Reanie was a good size woman, sweet as she could be, beautiful brown skin and some of the thickest black hair you'd ever see. Aunt Kate, "Everybody knows Rean loves her liquor and her man, why would Sarah try to mess with him?"

Doris, "Because she thinks her shit don't stink, because she's yellow. You know she always has to mention her color, I don't care if you talkin' about the price of rice."

I added my two cents "Reanie not only gave her want she wanted, she gave her what she needed. Quite a few folks have wanted to kick her ass for some time now."

I think I heard a car horn. I headed for the door, all excited, "I can't wait to see Sherrie's new car, she has a Mustang," I yelled from the front door.

Junie, Allen and Taz beat Mom, Aunt Kate and Poppa to the door to see this chick with the new sports car. It's still dusk outside so we can see the car pretty well. Allen and Junie are looking the car over and slapping Sherrie five. Meanwhile, little sis Taz is admiring the car and Sherrie's afro. I could see it in my little sister's eyes. That she was amazed at this dark brown skinned sister, smoking her cigarette dressed in a white outfit hip huggers and a matching halter covering her rather ample breasts, with the big afro and the brand new white Mustang with the black convertible top. She always thought Sherrie was cool, but this sealed it. My brothers also have new pretty sport cars, as do all the guys they hang out with.

Sherrie and I were saying, "See ya later", Allen was telling us he'll be to Big Bill's later, probably. I know he'll be there with his boys. So off we go to pick up Dasia and Anna.

Where I lived there were quite a few nightclubs to go to, we live near the shore resort area. We arrived at Bill's around eleven p.m., there were so many cars we almost couldn't find a parking spot. In all actuality, we all lived within one block from here, we could have walked and it would have been easier, but for Christ's sakes then people wouldn't have seen the new ride. James Brown is on as we make our way into the club, it's hot in here tonight I could feel the energy, we're immediately asked to dance as soon as we make our way to the dance area. I guess I'll have to get my drink after I make this cutie sweat a bit. Finally, after I'd almost perspired my hair back I headed for the bar, it took a little more to make that cutie sweat than I thought it would.

"Marie, over here - we've got a table", called Dasia.

Everybody and their momma, and daddy was here. I knew it, by 12:10 a.m. here's Allen, JoJo, and Dave (Dave's our cousin). JoJo and Dave two dark chocolate fine soul brothers, the three of them were tasting the treats, and flirting their way around the place, when Dave's ass was snatched onto the dance floor by his girlfriend - guess he wasn't expecting her to be in the bar.

After a night of shaking, swinging and grinding everybody said their good-byes and see ya tomorrows, then Allen and I decided to walk home, which is just around the block.

Allen said, "Man, this air feels kind of good. Did you hear that jive they were talking in there?

I was like, "Can you believe it I thought they were supposed to be friends."

Allen said, "Man that shit was crazy. They say a drunk man speaks a sober man's mind. If that's true, he was thinking some fucked up mess."

After our ten minute stroll home, we walked in the front door I could see the television on in the den. Allen calls out to Poppa, "Hey Pop, you feeling okay," and took a seat on the sofa. My Poppa, works for the Department of the Army, which required him to work swing shifts. He'd only been home a short while, that's why he was up so late tonight.

"Hi Poppa, see you in the morning," as I give him a kiss on the cheek. We're a kissy, huggy family. My Grandparents taught us to show love while the person is alive, not to wait until they pass away, and then say I loved him or her.

I'm exhausted, I mean truly exhausted. As I was taking my clothes off and getting ready for bed, I could hear Allen and Poppa downstairs talking about the day that just past, what was on television and some of everything else. As I faded from today's activities and begin dozing, I begin dreaming of Mike, soon I thought, soon.

Morning came so suddenly, it was around 8:30 a.m. when I opened my eyes, to run in the shower, which is so conveniently located right next to my bedroom. My God, it's a beautiful day outside, I thought to myself, as I got dressed. Junie headed for the bathroom, then while dashing down the steps he said, "See you at Grandma's and Grandpa's."

By the time I got dressed in my bright yellow sundress and put on my face, Allen began taking his shower, got dressed and was also leaving for Grandma's and Grandpa's too. I'm the last out the house, everybody else is already at Delia's and Robert's (grandma and grandpa). It's only a half a block to get there. Remember I told you we all live close by. Well, their backyard and driveway was full of their children, grandchildren, nieces, nephews, brothers and sisters. Let me tell you we have a big family. The smell of fresh coffee, biscuits, bacon, eggs, fried apples and grits filled the air as I started walking up the steps of the back porch. Everybody's greeting each other hugging, kissing, talking, and laughing just stomp down enjoying themselves. We got to laughing at how Reanie had beat Sarah's butt now it's even funnier, cause Reanie is telling and showing us what went on at the Green Briar.

"Marie, sweetie, you and Junie go out next to the chicken house and bring Grandma, all the eggs in the box", Grandma told us.

Dave and Allen were snickering and glancing at us. Junie said to me, "Come on and don't act stupid."

Off we go to the back of the yard. "You pick up the eggs, while I hold the basket", said Junie.

"No, I'll hold the basket you get the eggs. I don't want to touch the chickens, you know that", I barked at him.

While we were getting the eggs I asked him about his night. Lord, these chickens are all around us strutting and pecking about I'm scared of anything with feathers.

"So last night, what did you get into, or should I say who did you get into?"

"Fran and I went to the drive in", Junie told me.

"What did you see?" I asked.

"Some movie that was a suspense thriller", Junie said.

"How was it?"

"Fran or the movie?" he asked back.

I answered, "The movie nasty ass?"

Smiling showing those pretty teeth of his, he said, "The movie was pretty good from what I saw of it."

These chickens were getting too close to me, I started yelling and jumping all around, then one of them hopped off it's nest onto my head. "Help, oh my God help me!" I start flinging my arms all around, "Get them off me, help!"

Junie put the basket down and got the chicken off my head, meanwhile they were getting a laugh from me and the chicken. Well, anyway after being attacked by the chicken, Junie and I made our way back to the house so we could give thanks for our family, friends, food, and enjoy ourselves.

Now don't get me wrong, my life at this point might sound peachy right now, but our family has their problems, believe me. Sometimes my parents fuss and fight, Poppa running the streets, coming home beating on Momma just like a lot of other men. I just can't get into all of that now, it would take a story in it's self. I don't want you to get an unreal picture of us, so don't want you thinking we live on the sunny side of the street all the time.

Anyway, time is moving on, I guess it's been about two weeks since the attack of the chickens. So I'm at Grandpa's and Grandma's house with Aunt Kate just hanging out as usual, Grandpa and Grandma had gone to some friends' house for dinner. Grandma and Grandpa came in Grandma said she wasn't feeling good, so we tried to help her and make her feel better. Afterwards, I'd say about an hour or two later I went back down the street home, later that night Aunt Kate called to tell us Grandma is not doing well at all, she's going to the hospital. I told my Mom what Aunt Kate had just said, and the family went right down to their house, Grandma didn't want to go in an ambulance, said she's not feeling that bad, let's just go in the car. Everybody piles into their cars and off we go to the hospital. I was praying to God, "Lord please let Grandma be okay."
We're all talking and praying for Grandma to be fine. Later that night we all went home except Grandpa, he stayed at the hospital with Grandma. The next day my Grandmother past away, come to find out she had walking pneumonia. It broke my heart, not to mention all of my families' hearts, Grandma was the backbone of our family.

One of the sweetest, gentlest ladies, and she had such a good sense of humor, always saying or doing something to make you laugh. She kept us very close to her and each other. My Aunt Kate was extremely strong through this, no tears shed, my mother on the other hand was just the opposite, my uncles were so close to Grandma they absolutely didn't know what to do with themselves. When Momma and Poppa first got married, Momma was always at her parents' house, when Poppa got home from work he'd come to Grandma's and Grandpa's for dinner or Grandma would make a pan of biscuits to send him. Poppa had always swore she was one the sweetest ladies in the world.

Well, we all went to Grandma's funeral. People came from everywhere, my grandparents knew quite a few people. Afterwards all the people that were at the service went back to Grandpa's. I stuck close to Momma, she was having a hard time. Aunt Kate took care of everything, and everybody during this time. I was thinking, things are going to change I can feel it.

Within the next few weeks, Aunt Kate shut down, totally depressed, not thinking clearly, forgetting things. Whether it had just happened a couple of minutes ago or a couple of days ago, or she'd do things and not even know it or remember at all. This went on for some time, she finally had to go to the doctor's for help and took time off from work to get herself together.

As the saying goes time heels all wounds and makes it easier. I prayed to God this is true, because this is the hardest thing I can remember this family going through. When family members moved up here from down south, it was just natural and expected that they'd stay with my Grandma, she'd take all the family in and help them, no questions asked, just giving love, pure love, and never wanted anything in return, except for you to be a good person.Grandma's left us physically, but she's still with us forever.

Now in this letter, Mike is saying he can't wait to see me when he comes back to Jersey. I was so surprised to find out, he and his family are from South Jersey, mean while I'm from Central Jersey. This is going too smooth to be true.

May 1965

> *Michael Fazmen*
> *P.O. Box 162*
> *APO, NY 10021*

Dear Marie,

I hope this letter finds you well and happy.
It was a hard and busy day in the field, there's so much going on most of the time.

Anyway, time is passing not quick enough, and I can't wait to see you. So much to talk about when we're face to face.

Are you as excited and nervous as I am? Hope your family is not disappointed and more so I hope you're not disappointed when we meet. I don't when this day will be, but I'm dreaming of this day.

You had mentioned if I thought my feelings were just an infatuation because of the conditions of how we met. No, it's no infatuation for me, check to make sure of your feelings.

It's quiet now, so I'm gonna turn in and get some sleep.
Keep me in your prayers, cause you are always in mine.

Love,
Mike

That letter and telephone calling thing had gone on for
quite some time, I'd say about another eight months,
before he sends word that he's coming home soon. It's
hard trying to prepare yourself for something like this,
without working your nerves up. Its even harder hoping
for things to be right, with someone you haven't really
spent time with. I mean day to day living, getting to know
when or if he's moody, if he's actually neat or sloppy,
what his thought patterns are like in certain situations, is
he a nut? Just because I'm young and don't having a lot of
experience, I still know it takes a lot to make a relationship
work, so image what it would be like in my situation. I
don't know if people notice anything different about me,
but inside I feel somewhat jittery, anxious to see him, yet
maybe I'm actually nervous about it. In our letters and
phone conversations we've talked of being together, but
hey, I know men. Remember, I have two brothers and
my Poppa schooling me. I'm just gonna take one day at
a time, don't count on or expect anything. Also, Poppa
said a man will say anything to get what he wants. These
are a few things that I've learned.

"Marie it's almost time for you to go to work", called
Mom. "I know, how can I forget. Junie, I'll be ready in a
few minutes." It's Sunday night close to 10:15 p.m., Junie
and I work the night shift at a hospital. Then again some
of our relatives and friends also work there, of course
not all on the same shift. "Come on", Junie yelled up the
stairs. Running down the stairs, I called out "Ready, my

goodness we have plenty of time to get there." This is my last week on nights, Junie would be going to the day shift in three weeks.

Allen................

It was a late Saturday afternoon, just Junie and I were home, Pop was out and so was Marie. Mommy and Taz had gone down the street to Uncle C's house. So it was nice and quiet in the house for a while. Junie was in the kitchen, I was upstairs when I heard the front door get ripped open and I heard Taz crying like she was really hurt. I could hear her running through the house as she cried, so I jumped up and ran down the stairs as fast as my legs would carry me. Junie was calling for me, as I entered the kitchen Junie had sat her down on a chair right beside the doorway. I slammed on breaks and turned towards them, she was looking at us through her tears and panting for air, I was shocked to see her mouth and chin covered with blood. I grabbed the refrigerator door and tore it open to get some ice to put to her mouth, meanwhile Junie had his hand over her mouth. When I went to put the ice on her mouth I realized he wasn't just holding her mouth, he was holding her teeth in her gums. There were little pieces of gravel stuck in the front of her upper gum. We needed something cold that would cover her teeth and gums to stop the bleeding. We had always told her, that eating fudge pop sickles would turn her brown skinned like us, so she liked fudge pops, and kind of hoped it would turn her skin brown. Junie and I seemed to think of that at the same time, so he continued to hold her teeth in place, as I ran full speed out the front door and down the street to the corner store. I hoped nobody was coming out the door as I pushed through it and headed straight for the freezer section calling to

Jimmy the store owner, "Put two pop sickles on my tab, I'll be back to pay you" as I flung the store door open. I was running down the street like I had stole something, but I continued flying back up the street to Junie holding in our little sister's teeth. The bleeding had slowed down a little with the ice being held to her gums. I tore the paper from the fudge sickle and placed it in her mouth and told her to bite down. Junie said to her not to eat it, just almost bite through it and hold there. We were bent down to her so we could see what was going on in Taz's mouth. Almost through the whole fudge sickle and the bleeding was about to stop, we continued to follow the same procedure with the second piece of ice cream, because we had to make sure her teeth would be stable. So far this was working to slow the bleeding, now we began cleaning the pebbles from her gums.

After we'd taken care of her dilemma, we told her not to eat anything she had to bite using her front teeth.

By now Mommy had just come in the front door to see if Taz was here and see why she had left and come home without telling her. My brother and I explained what had happened to her mouth, Mom checked Taz over to make sure she was fine. Later after we were able to relax again, Taz told us how she had been on our cousin's bike and the handlebar was loose. When she rode up in a driveway to make a turn the handlebar went all the way forward and she fell over the handlebar onto the gravel on her mouth.

We had fixed Taz up and things around the house had quieted down this Sunday night, now it was almost time for bed when I said to Marie and Junie, "So ya'll be joining me on days next week, let me tell you, you'll be busier than you might expect. Between the patients and the administrators, I don't know who's worst. Anyway, I have four weeks to go then I'm on vacation for a week.

So you better enjoy working with me for the next few weeks."

Marie, "None of us even work in the same department."

"Just knowing you're on the hospital grounds the same time as me, should give you some sort of satisfaction", Allen said.

Monday came and went so as the rest of the week, and again this ritual was repeated.

Allen said, "It feels odd us riding in together. Marie you nervous about meeting Mike?"

Marie, "Hell yeah I'm nervous, cause actually I don't know what to expect or really what to do."

"Well first of all, he's got to meet and pass my inspection. Then we can take it from there, as for what you should do. How about Junie and I give you, say forty-five minutes to be alone and talk some, just enough time to start to break the ice, then gradually the family will drift into wherever you and Mike are."

"Then Junie and I will take him to hang out with us for a few hours. You know the guys can see him clearer, because they're men. We'll bring him back around six thirty or seven o'clock. You spend some more time with him, then we'll get a couple of people together and go out."

As I dropped Marie off at her cottage, the corniness came out of her, "See ya at three, it'll be you, you and me", she said pointing to me as she said this pathetic rhyme.

I was like, "Whatever see ya."

The person Junie was replacing on the day shift left their position a week early, so he was able to start sooner than was planned, this was a good thing.

We had finished another workweek and it's three ten p.m. Friday, by the time Junie and I picked up Marie.

"On the way home I have to pick up some clams. Anybody need to make any stops?"

"Not me", said Junie.

"Me neither", Marie.

So on the way home I ran into the seafood market for a second and right back to the car.

Junie, "On second thought I'd better get some beer to go with those clams."

Marie, "And I'd better gets some corn on the cob to make this right."

We made two more stops on the way home, the liquor store and the produce stand.

Arriving home I said, "We all know the procedure, now follow through", in my captain's voice. So as I put the clams in the sink to wash off and soak, Marie shucked the corn, put it in a nice big pot and seasoned it, while Junie located our little sister. Who is always busy and leaving the yard, which has a gate around it to keep her in the yard, but obviously it doesn't work, located Mom and Pop, and then gave Aunt Kate and Grandpa a call to check on them.

Finally, Mom, Dad and little sister had joined us as, we all made it to the kitchen table for dinner. Afterwards, "Dinner was delicious" Pop said as he went to get another cold one(beer) that is from the refrigerator.

"I'm so full I hurt, I'm going to have to sleep this off", as I almost waddled into the den to get on the sofa, we all headed for different rooms in the house to take it easy and unwind. I guess it was about eight thirty p.m. when I thought I should get up before I miss the whole night. As I continued to lay on, instead of getting up, the sofa the telephone rang, Junie answered the telephone, "Hey, how are you? It'll be nice to meet you, see you when you get here. Hold on, let me get her for you. Marie, telephone."

Marie took the phone "Hello, oh my God it's good to hear your voice. It's Mike everybody - Poppa, come say Hello.

Everybody spoke to him except me and Taz, I was just feeling too relaxed to move from the sofa with this fan blowing across me. Mommy said, "Look at her, she's all smiles and blushing."

Marie got back on the phone with Mike, "Uhm uhm, I thought about that too. You really think so. So you'll be here in a week, next Friday you'll arrive here at my house. You're going home to your family first, you'll get there Thursday morning around eight a.m.. Look sweetheart are you really gonna call me when you get home and see all your family? You'll be so excited. Stop it, you say you'll be more excited to see me. I'm excited too and so nervous. What would you like to do? Nasty thing! Really what and where would you like to go? Are you staying over night? There's so much to cover in a day. Am I asking enough questions or what? Oops! That was another question, I'm getting ahead of myself, let me calm down. Well, you think about what you'd like to do. Talk to you again Thursday and I'll see you Friday around five. We'll be waiting for you. The whole clan that's who. Have a safe trip, love you too", Marie finished her conversation with Mike.
I said, "Man, Friday'll be here in no time. You haven't met him yet, and you said you love him?" Everyone acted like I hadn't said anything and went about their way.

Wednesday evening about five I left to pick up Trina for dinner and a movie. When I came home I was telling Junie how Trina and I really had a good time and she has a great sense of humor, she is going back to Virginia next Wednesday, but we're going to keep in touch Trina was spending a week in Virginia before being set to her new post in Texas. We'd made plans for Saturday, Sunday and Tuesday, because she's expecting to leave next Wednesday, but the military never tells you the true date or location for security reasons, they'll wait until the last minute and tell you to pack up we're shipping out. I spent most of my time with coffee and cream the upcoming week, she was everything wrapped in one package.

Time was starting to go by too fast, so I figured I should get a start on getting some things together to take with me when I leave for basic training. This shit is scary, more than likely I'll end up in Vietnam. I mean literally in Vietnam fighting for my country. More important to me, is that I'll be fighting for my life and my sanity. Man, my cousin Dave is already gone, he's in North Carolina. The only good thing that might come out of this is Trina's going to Texas so I'll get to see her again.

My father used to say to us when we were small, "Set over there and let me look at you for a while". Now we're both looking at each other, whether we're setting around or moving about, I'll catch him watching me and vice versa. I'm going to miss my family, you know we're close. My Mother's planning a going away party for me, I swear she's the best mother in the world. I guess I might as well, drop coffee and cream a letter before I go to bed. I'm all into the letter I'm writing Trina, Junie started telling me how Paula was pushing him to go steady. I was expecting that. She'd already told me she intended to marry him.

Junie said, "I really like her, but I'm not quite ready for commitment. I'm not trying to do all that yet."

"Let her know where you're coming from. Man, she's into you for sure, she's a sweet kid. Just tell her you want to take things slow," I told him.

"I know that, but when she's looking at me with those big brown eyes I can't get it out, but I'm gonna have to tell her," Junie was telling me.

"The sooner you tell her, the better" I said.

"Yeah, yeah, I'm going to tell her next time I talk to her," said Junie.

Junie went on getting ready for bed.

"See you in the morning," Junie and I told each other as we started to fall asleep.

Sunday morning rolled around Mom, Aunt Kate, and Grandpa went to church. A little later, Mom and Aunt Kate returned around noon, Pop was out with his boys. So Mom and Aunt Kate went down to Grandpa's. I turned on the stereo and played some records, a quiet Sunday came and left. Monday, Tuesday, Wednesday came and my poor big sister was a ball of nerves.

Marie............

"Leya really you're usually here anyway, but just make sure you're here Thursday around five or five thirty to try and get things together, including me."

Leya, "Girl, your mom knows she can make some biscuits", as she finishes off a biscuit almost dripping of butter, "is there any chicken and gravy left, Tim and I are going to the movies, you wanna go?"

"No, I replied "I have quite a bit to do and I have too much nervous energy to sit through a movie. Ya know? I think I'm going to work a half day Friday, come home do some last minute things and take a break hopefully a nap, before he gets here."

Leya, "Can you believe we're finally gonna meet the voice? Well, girl gotta go, but I'll call you tomorrow. Calm down man, see you Thursday, that is tomorrow evening around five, alright?"

Finally, I made it to bed, let me just write these few things I'll have to do tomorrow. Okay that's done, lights off. Oh, let me just jot this one thing down so I won't forget. For the last time tonight now really lights out. My night of dreaming, catnaps, thinking, tossing and turning and then I turned and tossed some more.

Thursday morning I dragged myself from my bed. The ride to work was kind of quiet. Junie, "Looks like somebody had a hard time last night."
Tomorrow's the day", I replied. "That's all I kept thinking. What will it be like, will he be disappointed, will I be disappointed?"
Allen, "Hey if all else fells, at least it's an adventure."
"I'm gettin' off early today Leya's picking me up, don't forget."

Junie................
I'm just watching Sis (Marie) getting things together, trying to be relaxed Leya and Tim showed up just before five o'clock.
Tim, "Hey man, what's going down?"
"This nice cold beer is going down and fast, come on in the back yard, the guys are out here Pop's on the grill, getting ready for tomorrow. This weekend the gathering's here. Almost every weekend my family gets together for food, fun, drinks, dancing, and cards. Man, we travel between Massachusetts to North Carolina."
Tim is giving a shout to all and got a beer from the cooler.
"Allen, what's goin' on?"
Allen yelled back, "Yo man, just shootin' the breeze. Bring me that huge pot."
Tim, "Where you want it?"
Allen, "Throw it on the grill."
Everybody's a little busy. Uncle Ed, Uncle Jed, and Pop make some of the best homemade wine. "Joe take a sip to Marie and Leya on your way in. Mom and Aunt Kate probably could use one too, just looking at the other two run around."
Anyway, I was saying, everybody had a grapevine in their yard for the art of wine making. Ours was huge, it went up and over a wooden frame made to support

the vine to grow on, underneath was outdoor furniture, a hammock and a swing set, about twenty feet behind this is a little house, we call it that, because it was actually a secondary house for us. When you take a step up into the door to your left is the pantry with a freezer, shelves and a counter, across from the freezer is a window with some cute little curtains my mom made, behind this room is my Dad's work room every kind of tool you'd probably think of is here along with his work bench, then there's the main room the size of the other two rooms together. This room has two windows up high about two feet in height and about five feet in length. There's a corner where the wine jugs are stored waiting for the wine to age, next to that stash is a bookshelf from the ceiling to the floor filled with National Geographics and encyclopedias. Dad likes nature, that's where all the National Geographics come in hundreds of them. An old taupe victorian looking sofa and chair, an end table, record player, and some of my little sisters toys. My Mom and Dad built this spot after adding the kitchen, powder room and bedroom to our main house.

Uncle Jed asked, "Allen did you get your date to report for duty?"

"No Unk, I imagine I will report to Ft. Worth, in Texas. It's scary, but exciting too in a way."

Uncle Jed said, "How bout you Tim, glad you did your bid an made it home, I know."

Tim, "Yeah, it wasn't as bad as I expected it to be, because of the company I was in, I didn't get to see much action, thank God. But some of the other cats, Lord knows experienced the worst of it, some didn't make it back and then there are others that came back home physically but their minds are shot out. Veterans came back home from a war they didn't even want to fight in and it's like society and the U.S. government have tossed them aside."

Marie.............

    We were sipping on a glass of wine sent in the house to us, and Leya is telling me, "You know you want to look unintentionally sexy."

"Yeah exactly, like I'm not trying to look sexy," I said.

Well after fiddling around in my closet for a while she picked out an outfit for me to wear and it looked just right.

"Girl what would I do without you", I said to her.

Then hearing all the laughing coming from the backyard, I went into my parent's bedroom where one of the windows overlooked the yard.

I said to Leya, "Come on let's go outside and see what's going on." So I grabbed my wine and off we went down the stairs and out the back door.

"Play that record again Junie, so I can finish shakin' my thing," Aunt Kate said, and so they played it again so Mom and Aunt Kate could finish shakin' their thing. I joined right in to James Brown latest hit, Allen put down the potholder he was wearing

on his hand and came on over to join in the dance too. We all danced for some time, Allen and me, Allen and Momma, and Allen and Aunt Kate - oh I'd say we danced a good thirty minutes, even worked up a sweat. Poppa was cooking up a storm on the grill, so actually our cookout had already gotten started. Everybody ate and hung around for a short while, but cleared out by I'd say about nine-thirty that evening. You know it was a Thursday night, and everybody had to make it to work the next day.

    After everyone had left Momma and I talked about the up coming day and how she wanted me to stay close by, because we don't really know Mike. I had to admit I thought that was a good idea too, not only for that reason, but because it would help me not to be so nervous. Plus I knew he'd have a good time here with my family. If he couldn't have fun with us, then he just was not capable of having fun.

Well I decided I'd better get ready for bed, because I was tired and sleep, but at the same time wired. I was a ball of nerves trying to convince myself to please get some sleep. Lord, please make me to go to sleep soon, so I will be alert tomorrow and not have bags big enough to be full blown luggage sets under my eyes tomorrow, I prayed. Okay, I had finally gotten ready for bed and climbed in between my nice cool fresh feeling sheets. You know that sensation, when you're tired and the sheets feel as though they're caressing your legs and feet when you get in? "Uhm."
Oh yeah, I forgot one thing, so I got out the bed to run to the bathroom to make sure my stockings were hanging up to dry, just in case I needed them over this weekend. Back to bed I went, then one more thing before I shut my eyes, so I got up to take care of that. Just small things that might add up, you know? All right finally everything is taken care of, so I got in my bed for the night now, then I tossed and I turned, I turned and I tossed, and so on and so on.

Friday morning and the sun was coming up, I figured I could use a few more winks. And so I took another little nod until about eight-thirty a.m. When I awoke, I felt nice and refreshed, God had given me a good nights sleep. As I put on my robe and went down the stairs, I headed for the kitchen and saw the back door open-Poppa was outside working in his garden and picking tomatoes. Everybody else had gone to work. "Good mornin' Poppa," I called to him from the kitchen door.
"How you doin' baby," Poppa called back.

"Pretty good, how about you," I asked.

He said, "Come and get you some of these tomatoes, they're beauts."

That's short for beauties. I do have to mention my father has been in the newspaper a couple of times for his prize-winning tomatoes. So I got the salt and went out to the garden where I could have a field day with the tomatoes. I picked a few, washed them off and set two of the rocking chairs close to Poppa one for each of us, so we could talk and eat a few of his beauts. Then we went in the house, so Poppa could peel a few tomatoes to eat with our breakfast, I cooked us some eggs, bacon, and toast. And then it was on.

I wasn't even expecting one of my girls to come by early today, but Desia was here by one o'clock, boy was I happy to see her. She wanted to know if I needed anything, I told her, "No everything's been taken care of, but just keep me company."

We were sitting there watching our soap opera, The Guiding Light, advising the characters what to do and fussing them out, when my telephone rang. Did you guess who it was calling me? It was Mike, telling me he wouldn't be able to make it, I started to get upset, but something said play it cool. "Are you for real", I asked him? Then that fool said, "I'm just playin', see you in a few."

After I hung up the phone, I felt a bit more nervous.

Junie............

Finally, it's Friday, it's payday, we're gonna have a ball tonight, and one more thing we're gonna actually meet this Mike tonight. "Hey man, get in," I called to Allen as he was already opening the car door of my black Super Sport.

"To the bank, my good fellow, and I shall pay ye for thoust troubles," Allen said. Then off we headed for the bank.

We got home our usual time on paydays, which was about quarter after four p.m., we had some time to unwind a little, before people started coming over. We did a few small finishing details around the house, nothing fancy, just making sure we had enough ice, sodas, putting some things where they'd be easy to get to, things like that.

I'd say it was about five-thirty that evening, my mother and Aunt Kate were sitting in the living room, when the doorbell rang. My mother was answering the door as Marie came down the stairs. We knew Marie had to be nervous, but she was acting smooth as she went to the door, where her guest had just stepped in. They both were grinning and smiling enough for us to see every tooth in their mouth. They greeted each other with an affectionate yet conservative or cautious hug.

Marie.............
Everybody this is Mike, and so I introduced him to Junie, Mom, and Aunt Kate, then I took him in the back yard to meet my father and Allen. The conversations were going well as we talked with everybody, a little later Mike and I had some time by ourselves, but even then we just talked and talked and admired each other. By this time company started drifting into the backyard, so I excused myself for a minute to go put some records on the record player. I needed to step away from him for a minute to give my tired cheeks a break from smiling and to breathe again.

When I finally made it back to Mike after about ten minutes, he was talking with a group of people with his fine ass self. I'm telling you everything was going so well,

I felt high. Speaking of high I got myself a drink, Mike already had a non-alcoholic drink in his hand. As the night went on we all danced, drank, ate, and laughed our asses off. As you can tell - the plan my brothers had about taking him out with them for a few hours fell through, everybody was here and they liked him. But still within the next few days I was still going to have Allen and Junie spend some time with Mike away from the house.

By about two o'clock in the morning the front yard and back yard were beginning to empty. "Good night", "Talk to you tomorrow", "Be careful going home", was coming from all over the yard, and thank God almost everything in the yard had been cleaned up, I didn't feel like spending my last few waking moments tonight cleaning when you know what I had rather been doing. That's right, no shame in my game, Mike and I rode to the beach and parked facing the ocean. I was saying to myself when is this man going to kiss me, I'm trying to be a good girl (hum) and let him make the first move, but if he keeps this up, I'm gonna snatch him by his collar and lay these hungry lips on him. He finally made his move, he leaned over in the middle of one of my words and he kissed me. It was a nice soft slow kiss, it was all I was hoping for, it was real nice. Not too aggressive, and not too passionate, but it let me know there would be more to come. So we kissed a little more, the way he rubbed my thigh I could tell he was excited about this new territory. Then we caught our breath, straightened our clothes, and drove back to my house, the car was quiet most of our ride. You know like, when in the car is silent, but it's not a tense silence, it was a content silence, with a promise of more to come. A promise, of more what to come? You better act like you know.

We pulled up in front of the house and not only was the house dark, all the entire neighborhood houses were dark. Mike came around to my side of the car and opened the door for me to get out. As I put my legs out the car my dress slid up about two inches, I don't know if it just happened or if I had done that on purpose.

He was standing so close to me when I stood up out of the car I had to squeeze between his body and the car to get past him. We made into the house and I told him to make himself at home and reminded him where the bathrooms were then asked him to pull out the sofa bed while I got the linen to make his bed. I went upstairs to get the linen and when I came back downstairs, he wasn't in the den, I heard the powder room door open and close. Looking in my eyes, he walked in my direction bare chest and barefoot he stopped right in front of me and proceeded to lay his shirt on the arm of the sofa, the whole while I was watching his every move.

"So what's up for later today?" he asked.

"Remember I told you to think of something you wanted to do. Did you?" I said back.

"Let's go to the beach for a while, so I can see it during the day", Mike said.

"Sounds good to me. Have a good night." I told him, then I gave him a peck on his lips.

Mike said, "Good night, but it would be better if we were sleeping together."

I pretended I hadn't heard his reply, but I thought to myself as I went up to my bed, you ain't never lied.

Everybody slept later than normal the next morning, when Momma and Papa went downstairs, they told Mike to get in their bed to finish sleeping, "Take your pillows on up there with you," Momma told him.

I guess it was about eleven that morning when I opened my eyes and went to Allen and Junie's room, just to find they weren't in there. I heard something behind me, looked back to find Mike. "Oh, you scared me, have you seen my brothers? Why were you in my parents bedroom?"

"First, no I haven't seen your brothers, and second, your mother told me to go to her room to finish sleeping. Good morning to you too, Love," Mike answered.

"Good morning," was all I could say and smile. "I'm trying to find my brothers to get some friends together to go to the beach with us."

From the top of the stairs, I called downstairs, "Junie - Allen."

I could hear everybody else downstairs, Junie answered me, "What?"

"We wanna go to the beach this afternoon, let's get some people together" I yelled down to him.

"About what time," Junie called back from the bottom of the stairs.

"Say, two o'clock," I said.

"Will do, even if I'm not here at that time just go down to Belmar and we'll meet there," Junie said.

"Alright," I said.

Turning back to Mike I said, "We better start getting ready, two o'clock will be here in no time."

Mike pushed my hair back behind my ear, then gently ran his finger down my neck before kissing me. I wanted to react to his touch, but I couldn't move. Afterwards Mike told me to go on and take my bath first. He went downstairs to the kitchen with everybody else to get a bite to eat. After I came out the bathroom, got dressed, and put on my make-up I went down to eat, then Mike went up stairs to clean himself up. Papa had gone out into the backyard to watch the birds that came to eat. Then we heard Papa and other voices in the yard, it was Grandpa. Mama and I went outside to join them.

A few minutes later Chocolate Dream(I'm going to call him in my mind)came outside and joined Grandpa and

Papa in the garden. He had told me he had grown up on a farm, come to find out he really had. He and Grandpa were talking like two old farmers and Grandpa was impressed. "That boy knows his stuff," Grandpa said.

A little past noon the telephone started ringing about meeting at the beach, I had called Leya, Desia, and Judy. Desia was calling me back to say she was going. She was looking forward to wearing some tiny bikini she'd bought last week. Desia and her date would be riding with us. Usually everybody brought something to the beach, you know like sodas, sandwiches (subs), fruit.

About one fifteen, in the afternoon, Allen came in from the night before. "Where have you been all this time," I asked?

"Out. What's goin' down", he said.

"Well, we're going to the beach about in about fifteen minutes, you gonna make it?

Allen replied, "Yeah might as well, let me get my stuff and a quick bite."

As soon as Allen disappeared to get his things, Junie ran in the door.

Mama was getting Taz's things together, so we could take her with us. My brothers too her with them a lot, the basketball court, dates, just kept her hanging around them. It might seem kind of unusual for young men to have a little sister hanging around them because they enjoyed it, but these two liked having her around. I'll admit I spent quite a bit of time with her also, but I'm a female. Anyway back to what I was saying. You know I'm thinking, was having her around some kind of girl magnet. Lord knows they had plenty of beautiful women swarming around them. Anyway, Taz was riding with Junie and Allen, like most times. It was a hot sunny day, and I do mean hot. We found our spot some of our friends were there already and set up. It was on, we played football, and swam.

Okay, I didn't swim, I was just sticking my feet in the water, when somebody picked me up and ran with me screaming, kicking and almost crying out into the water. There were other people around us in the water, but I kept my eyes on my brothers running close by and laughing. I was calling to them for help, my God we went further and further out in the water. The beach had become an uproar of laughter and screaming. Next thing I know we stopped and I was dunked, but these strong arms were still holding me while I was under the water. Damn it, Mike was the ass that took me out there into what seemed like the middle of the Atlantic Ocean. When I finally got back on the sand it hadn't been too too bad. That's when I saw my brothers out in the middle of the Atlantic with some of our friends. Well I knew my brothers wouldn't have let things get too out of control while Mike was acting a fool with me. I have to be honest, I couldn't even stay mad at Mike, for one thing he was looking so damned good standing there soaking wet, with his six foot four inches sculpted muscular body, pretty teeth and sexy almond shaped eyes with the water running from his hair, down his face. I swear by the end of this beach day I was tired and needed some solid food in my stomach.

Allen...........

"Speaking of solid food, that would be on the money right now. Sandwiches are nice and all, but you know what we were raised on. Heavy solid food, that's right. I'm gonna get Taz she's playing at the edge of the water," I was saying. I went and got her, "Come on little girl let's go home, I'm starving and I'm tired."
Junie was getting our stuff together, saying he had somewhere to be later. I said, "Man I'm not going anywhere tonight, guess it'll be me, Taz, some junk food and the

2 222252224273222228

television tonight, I was saying. Then I asked, "Who are you going out with?"

Junie said, "No date tonight just hanging out."

When we reached the house I can say, I was never so glad to get home, I cleaned my plate, and then it took everything I had, to make it to the sofa in front of the fan. I layed at one end little sis sat at the other end. Next thing I knew I woke up and it was dark outside and Mom was on the loveseat across from me. I went in the kitchen to get my junk food supply, scooter pies and milk. While I almost ate my first one whole, Taz was eating hers with a method, the top layer of cookie, the bottom layer of cookie and last but not least the marshmallow.

Junie and Joe came through the den on their way out. As Joe was picking on Taz he asked me, "You sure you not coming?"

"Man, I'm sure, this is the hot spot for me tonight," I said.

Junie gave Mom and Taz a goodbye kiss. Mom, Taz and I watched television for a while, until Mom got Taz ready for bed around ten o'clock, but Taz returned back to her spot on the sofa, so we could watch scary movies on the late night movies.

Marie...............

Mike and I went for a ride later that night and ended up at the movies. Well one thing lead to another, like his caressing me and kissing my neck, and passion started to rise among other things and next thing I knew we were on our way to find a nice hotel. We found a nice hotel across the street from the beach. In the elevator I had to rub his chest and flat muscular stomach, he responded by stroking my hair and then by giving me one of the sweetest kisses. I swear he had pulled his lips away from mine, but I could still feel the softness of his lips and tongue. As we walked into the room the place was nice and cool, and almost everything in the room was white - shag rug, walls, two white leather chairs, a circular table in between them, and the bed was huge and the bedspread was lime green with large white polka dots. I removed my shoes as I always did as soon as I got inside. He took off his short sleeve shirt and shoes, strolled over to the bed, "Gotta test it you know," he said. "Come on, help me try it out."

Mike laid on his back looking up at the ceiling for a second, before he started rubbing my back, then he took me by the arm and pulled me to him. To be honest he didn't have to pull hard, then I think I started the kissing, first his cheek, neck, chest, licked his nipples, and moved down to kiss his stomach. "Let me go to the bathroom, I'll be right back," I told him.

When I returned from the bathroom Mike said he had called for room service. I picked up the telephone to call and tell Momma I wouldn't be home tonight.

"What did you order," I asked, walking over to the leather chairs to set down.

"I ordered some champagne, a plate of shrimp with coleslaw, and chocolate cake. Miss is that okay with you," he said?

I said, "I guess it'll have to do for now."

He walked over to the window facing the ocean and said, "Can you believe we're both from New Jersey and I had to go all the way on the other side of that ocean to fight in a war for us to meet?"

"The Lord had some mapped out plan for that one, but here we are finally," I said to Mike. Then I walked over to where he was standing still looking out at the ocean, and put my arm around his waist.

The doorbell rang and he went to get the door, of course it was our food. The man rolled the tray inside the door and proceeded to setup our eating places, plates, glasses, candles and all. Mike tipped the guy, and thanked him for the prompt service. I was lighting the candles, Mike turned off the lights and strolled back to the table and gave me a big hug. We sat at the table and started the celebration. First we took a sip of the champagne, then it was on to feeding each other shrimp and washing them down with the champagne. "Man, this is almost as tasty as you," said.
"I agree it's good, but let's not get stupid about it being almost as tasty as me. Maybe I'll have to let you get another sample of what I taste like, if you forgot that damned fast," I told him.

The ocean was singing a beautiful song, but I wanted to hear another song along with the ocean, so after a few minutes I suggested we turn on the radio. A song by the Four Tops was playing so we danced in front of the open window, feeling the fresh ocean breeze blow through the window. It was like I was dreaming, Mike turned the light off in the room, meanwhile the moon gave plenty of it's light through the windows. He came back in front of the window, where I stood, I was almost unable to move waiting to feel his body against mine. While we were dancing I felt his hand caressing my back, I kissed his chest a few times, then our lips met again, our hands began exploring each other, in a gentle yet excited way. We danced our way over towards the bed. Then I suddenly got so nervous, it dawned on me, this is going somewhere I've never been before. Should I sleep with this man? I want to sleep with this man. What will he think if I do, what will he think if I don't?
"Mike, I'm really nervous right now. I've. Well, I'm trying to say is that I've," I said.

"You're nervous, yeah, what else are you having so much trouble saying?" he asked.

"I've never gone all the way before, I finally got it out of my mouth," I told him.

"No problem, we don't have to, but I'd really like to, but it's up to you. I'm not going to force you." Mike was rambling on.

"Okay, let's take our time. Seems like you're nervous yourself, " I said.

"Me? No not really, a little maybe, you know," he said.

So I went to the bathroom, and started running the water to take a quick shower, when I heard a tap on the bathroom door. "Marie, I was thinking, we could take a shower together. It'll be fun and it'll take less time for us both to get cleaned up. I was naked so I wrapped a towel around myself and opened the door. "Come on in," I told him. The door opened, as Mike walked into the bathroom he was naked, he removed the towel from my body, took my hand as he lead us into the shower. He soaped the wash cloth and started on my back, worked his way around to the front of me and went from my neck to my breasts and stomach, down a little further to my happy place, where he paid special attention to this area, then down to my legs and my feet. In return I soaped the other wash cloth and began with his face, to his neck, on to his back down to his tight butt, and then the back of his legs. Then I moved to the front of him where I rubbed the soapy cloth on his chest and stomach, onward to his throbbing protrusion, down his legs and last, but not least his feet.

It had started all over again the yearning, the desire. Okay, I admit it yes, the love, the need to make love had gotten so strong. We dried each other's body and I kissed him on his chest, not just because it had become a comfortable place for me, but also because I couldn't reach his face without getting him to bend over some. We went back to the bed, where Mike pulled back the covers and we slid in between the sheets. We talked for all of a minute, before he began caressing my face and breasts, and of course, I caressed him back. One touch led to another, another, and the next thing we had become one. I don't know what time it was when we finally drifted off to sleep, but I slept like I had been sedated.

The day came and the sun shining in the window made me open my eyes, then I recognized the sound of the pounding ocean and the seagulls. Before Mike woke up I made it to the bathroom, where I got my clothes on when I walked back out the bathroom, he was awake. He was looking at me so, it made me nervous again. I'm thinking to myself, "What is he thinking?"
He said, "Morning, you feeling okay?"
"I'm fine, how about you?" I said, not looking at him.
"I see you took a shower without me," he said.
Then he got up and walked in the bathroom, I could hear him whistling as he moved around in there.
The bathroom door opened, he came over and gave me a kiss, "So what do you want to do today, pretty girl? Although, I hope it's not much."
"Taking it easy today is fine with me, we'll spend some time with your family since they'll be coming to my parents' for a visit later this morning. So let's just stay around the house today, alright?" I asked.
"That's a plan. Now let's go for a walk on the boardwalk, before we start our day. Normally I exercise early in the morning, this feels funny not exercising for the last couple of days, Mike said as he did a few stretches and yawns.

Well, close to an hour after Mike and I got back to my house his family pulled up, yeah two carloads of them. Look he has a large family, and I was enjoying them, but I swear I was so tired, and tomorrow I have to go to work. I just want to set down around six o'clock and relax until it was time to go to bed. I decided I'd better go into a quiet room to call my job and request the next day off, thank goodness I was granted a vacation day. I would need it to get some needed rest.

Mike had bought the Sunday paper to check out some things in the area. Was it me or was this going kind of fast, I was thinking to myself. A tiny little part of me was saying take it slow, but my heart and my body are saying hurry the hell up. Anyway, around eight that night, his family left to go back to south jersey. Mike stayed with me until the next morning, I was kind of glad he did. The next day Mike returned to south Jersey too, said he'd come up the following weekend.

My family and I had really enjoyed him and his family, our families hit it off big.

Our parents' had made plans to get together again within the next few weeks.

Allen............

Saturday we went to check out the NCO Club. I figured I might as well start getting familiar with going to military places, I knew my time was coming, the draft was going on big time. The Air Force is for intellectually bright individuals they say - therefore, my brother served in the Air Force and so will I.

Marie and I walked into the NCO Club, it was a nice place, large dance floor, lounge, beautiful chandeliers hanging from the ceiling, and they even served dinner. Making our way along side the dance floor through the crowd that was here to obviously have a good time, we spotted a vacant table over near the columns adjoining the lounge to the main room. "Oh yea, yea, I'll take a shot of Tangeray on the rocks with the rim salty and she'll have a screwdriver," I told the waitress.

Marie scooted over close to me, to tell me that girl's looking at me, but I'd already spotted the chick. Yes I have, because she's fine. She's coffee and cream complexion – heavy on the cream, bout 5'4, green eyes, body like a brick house, shoulder length hair that was as black as a crow. "You know damn well I spotted that right away." So Marie put her hand on my forearm, steadily running her mouth, I heard her, but at the same time I was surveying the club and keeping an eye glued on coffee and cream, while only letting her see a glance every now and then. "Here are our drinks", Marie said smiling at me.

Marie..............

This girl is so blatantly eyeing my brother, she doesn't know if we're dating, just friends, cousins, or sister and brother. So you know I performed a little just to keep her from getting bored.
"Allen let's dance," so now we're movin' it on the floor, whenever the dance requires me to get close I glance at her. Allen doesn't see what I'm doing. I can see it on her face, she thinks we're girlfriend and boyfriend. Eventually, Allen and I make it back to our table, when we returned we had been joined by El and Dave.

Allen............

"Hey man, glad you made it."
Dave said, "Come on girl let's dance?" Off Dave and Marie went to the dance floor.
"Man I got my eye on that girl."
"So what your wanting' for?" Elliot said, "Go talk to her. What's wrong you scared?"
"Me scared, yeah right. I'll be right back." So I stood up making sure I'm correct, and then I began my long

long journey across the room toward coffee and cream. As I stroll up on the side of her and bend down, "Excuse me, but you're beautiful. So I hope you'll excuse me for having looked at you so hard. I've finally gotten my nerve up to ask you to dance, so please answer yes."

She replied, "I think you should go back to your date, but thank you for the compliment."

"I'm not here with a date, that girl I'm with is my sister."

"She didn't give the impression of being your sister, maybe another time, okay?", she said.

So now I'm thinking oh no this girl is tripping, what is she talking about.

"By the way here she comes, have a nice night", she said.

Here comes Marie, wearing hot pants and high heeled sandals emphasizing her long shapely legs, large black curls bouncing and dancing all around her shoulders, and said, "Excuse me, is my brother bothering you?" Coffee and Cream looks at us with a bit of a strange look.

"I'm Marie, this is my brother Allen, is he bothering you? I apologize I didn't get your name."

"Oh hi, my name is Trina." coffee and cream replied.

"Now would you like to dance or could I buy you a drink or both?" I asked again.

"A dance would be nice." she said. Man she had made my night. Taking her hand we headed for the dance floor.

"I told you she was my sister," I said to Trina.

After a few songs we went outside to cool off, talk and exchange phone numbers. "So, my name is Allen, and you said yours is Trina. That name seems to fit you. What brought you out tonight?" She said she was in the army and was here for some kind of military reason, so the next thing I knew she's telling me why she decided to go into the army, what she does in the army, where she's from. And I'll be damned if she's not from Virginia, but her mother now reside in - you said it New Jersey, about forty-five minutes from where I live. I told her where I'm from, that I'm going in the Air force, the reason why I'm going into the military, which is because I was being drafted. I don't know, but I think being drafted is a good enough reason to go in. We exchanged phone numbers and I asked Trina to go out with me tomorrow. "Trina, I really enjoyed you with your permission, I'd like to see you again."

 Trina was like, "I enjoyed you also, so when would you like to see me again?"

I told her, "Let's say Friday evening around six thirty?" She nodded and smiled in agreement.

"Okay that sounds alright with me." So she gave me the info on how and where to reach her. Meanwhile, Marie, El, and Dave were coming out the NCO Club, we all said our good-byes, and I saw to her getting back inside to her friends and then I headed for the parking lot. Before I could get behind the wheel Dave was like, "So?"

Playing dumb, I'm like, "What?"

Dave, "So what's up, is she digging you?"

I say, "You mean physically or situation wise? See ya tomorrow man, if Laura let's you get calls or come out."

    It's now Sunday morning the breeze was soft and warm as it blew in throw our windows, light rain was beating against the windows and on the rooftop. Junie and I laid in our bed talking. Somehow while we were asleep little sis had squeezed in the bed and was listening like a grown woman. "Sounds like Grandma, Grandpa, and Aunt Kate are down stairs." Junie said. Taz got out the bed to go check it out for us. The family was downstairs all right, so I threw some water on me, then went downstairs to see everybody. We all spent the morning and half the early afternoon at our house, just relaxing and looking out the front door at the rain fall, and checking to see if anybody was stirring around outside.

Marie…………..

This weekend as usual Mike was coming up and he was joining the shore basketball team. When he mentioned joining I had asked him, won't that be a conflict of interest? You know your boxing, what if you get hurt while you're playing? He said he wouldn't get hurt, that's no problem. He was good at boxing, I thought if he pursued it wholeheartedly he'd get somewhere with it.

Mike was moving to Neptune within the next two weeks. He was planning on getting a room until we got married, yes married. Mike hadn't actually asked me yet, but I knew it was coming, because he'd mentioned a few plans he had for after he and I had gotten married.

Thursday, when I got home from work Mike was here. "I wasn't expecting you to be here today," I told him.

"Is there a problem with me being here today, you had other plans, hum," Mike said?

"No, it's no problem, just wasn't expecting you, but I'm glad to see you. How's the family," I asked.

He was standing there looking at me like, right. Anyway, I gave him a nice little kiss and a hug that broke his chill.

"What's going on with you moving," I asked?

Mike told me, "Next weekend my brothers are going to help me move. I don't have much to bring, so it won't take long. We figured with all of them driving their cars, we'd only have to make one trip."

The whole time he was telling me this he's trying to feel on me and to be honest I appreciated his attention. I mean I only got this on the weekends, but that won't be for much longer.

Saturday rolled around and I was feeling a little down. "Marie what's wrong," Mike wanted to know?
"I'm thinking about my brother leaving soon. I hope to God he makes it back home and gets to come home soon or better yet, the war will end before he leaves. That's the most important thing on my mind these days. Second, whose going to keep their eye on me like him?"
"Allen will make it home safe, plus he'll be in the Air Force. The Marines and the Army are on the front line, and as for whose going to watch you, that's where I come in," he said, smiling at me.
"Mike are you trying to flirt with me while I'm this find of a mood?" I asked.
"Yeah, I guess I am. You got a problem with that?" he said.
All I could was smile and give him a push on his shoulder.

This weekend Mike was so busy looking through the local paper, for jobs and apartments and anything else he could think of, us going out having fun was secondary this weekend. He left Sunday afternoon, in his new GTO, it was sharp, dark green with white interior.

Allen was spending a lot of his time home and at our Grandfather's. I could see he's worried, but at the same time he wanted to go and just get it over so he can come back home. Allen's motto is "expect the best, but prepare for the worst".
Yet he did have some time to spend with Trina, of course.

The week had flown by. Taz told Allen she wanted to buy a record. So he had told her he would take her to the record store Friday, she had gotten her two dollar allowance on Tuesdays and she was almost counting the minutes on Friday waiting for Allen to take her to the get this record she wanted. I was looking out the window when I saw Taz walking down the walkway beside our house toward Allen. He was waiting for her, he put her in the front passenger seat next to him, closed her door before he rounded the car and got in the driver's side and they headed for her to buy Ain't No Mountain High Enough, by the Supremes. We thought this was so cute, because she was only five years old, buying records.

That following Saturday Mike and his brothers pulled into town, me and my brothers went down to help them unpack their cars. Sherrie (is married to Mike's brother Rob) and I fried some chicken, made some potato salad and tossed salad for lunch, while two of the guys ran to the liquor store. After everything was finally placed inside, we turned it into a party. Leya, Dasia, Elliot, Ed, and Trina came over and it was on. We just played the stereo, danced, talked, drank and played cards until half the night was over.

You know then the time came for Mike and I to make our way out of there for some time alone. I was aching to feel him pressed against me. We went to the same hotel we'd stayed at before, because his brother Rob and Sherrie were staying the night at Mike's. This time was different than before, when he and I went to the hotel, I wasn't the same nervous girl as before, I at least had an idea of what I was doing. There was no question that he knew what he was doing. Mike stopped kissing on my neck to ask me, "Are you glad I moved up this way?"
"Of course I'm glad, we can spend more time together," I told him.
"I'm glad too, we can do this more often," then he continued to kiss my neck, shoulders, and down to my breasts, as I removed his shirt.

That following week Mike got a job with the department of sanitation, which was a good paying job, he joined a gym and the basketball team my brothers were on. He was really making a life here for himself. Everything was going fine for him.

Let's see, it's been a week since he moved here, I treated him to dinner for a change. We both loved seafood, so we went to the Lobster Shanty, a place Junie had schooled me on. It was a nice place on the marina, where the boats pulled right to the back doors, where the restaurants bought the seafood. It can't get any fresher than that.

Mike said, "There's something I have to ask you later."

"What is it you want to ask me?"

"I'll ask you later, don't worry about it," he said.

"That's crazy. You mention asking me something, now you gonna keep me in suspense", I said.

He says, "I didn't mean to do that, I just want you to know I'm going to bring something up a little later".

I just looked at him and shook my head.

We talked while enjoying dinner and afterwards we walked outside on the dock. "You know I've been wondering should we," he said and stopped.

I'm like ,"Should we what?"

"Well, I've been wanting to ask you would you marry me?" he finally said.

I had to step back a few steps so I could look at him real good and take in the whole picture that was going on here. "Did you say marry?"

All of a sudden he was so unsure of himself, which was so different, because usually he was a little arrogant.

"Yeah, I was wondering," he was saying again, but before he could even finish saying it, I answered, "Yes, I'll marry you."

I was all tears and smiles.

The next day we went and told our families we were getting married, they were all happy for us. Mike and my parents got along so well, his parents would come up for the weekends and visit with my parents and vice versa. Well, we'd set the date as soon as possible, because I wanted both my brothers to be there. Mike and I went and applied for our license and got the blood test done. Meanwhile, Aunt Kate and Momma were planning a small reception for us, at the house.

We got our blood test results back in about five days, then we got our license. Two days afterwards, we're standing in front of the preacher taking our vows, I was hoping I wouldn't break out into a sweat, I swear I was so nervous. So we had a very small wedding just our families at my family's church.

We got home and some of our friends were already waiting for us, throwing rice and they'd decorated the house inside. I admit it looked beautiful and I'm so excited and in love.

I was starting a new adventure, a new life with a new man and you know, I know it'll have it's ups and downs, but hey.

Grandpa said to us, "It would be nice if you two stay with me and your Aunt Kate until you get on your feet."

"Really Grandpa? I'd love for us to stay with you two, " I said, then I looked at Mike all excited, like come on this is going to be great staying with them. I was already living with Grandpa and Aunt Kate. After Mike giving his landlord a short notice Mike moved in with Grandpa and Aunt Kate three days later.

"How's everybody doing today," Mike said as he walked through the door from taking his physical for his new job. "Well ladies, I start my job with the township, I start this coming Monday."

"That's great Mike", Aunt Kate said to him and gave him a big ole hug. He picked Aunt Kate up and swung her around.

After her feet were back on the floor, Aunt Kate and I continued to fixing dinner, then Grandpa came in with Momma, and Uncle C in tow right behind him. Uncle C is the baby of the family, but Momma swears, she's still Grandpa's baby too.

"Daddy I made you some biscuits," Momma said to Grandpa, "Is dinner ready yet", Momma then asked us?

Aunt Kate replied, "It'll be ready in about half an hour."

Mike and I had discussed our ideas of how we thought our marriage should operate. One thing he requested was that I leave my job, because he preferred I take care of the house. I didn't find a problem with this request, I did a few heads of hair every now and then to make a little extra change.

As the days past, I admit things were going pretty well between Mike and I. We were saving money to get our own place, although Grandpa would constantly remind us there was no hurry. I thought he wasn't used to his house having such few people in it, that's why he encouraged us to stay here. Me myself, I love it here, but I know Mike and I will need our own space. Considering I just found out I was pregnant. I hadn't told Mike or anybody else yet. I knew I wasn't feeling just right, so I went to the doctor when my period didn't show up. Tell me this, is it strange that your man can tell you when your period is late or early. So yes, Mike had mentioned, when is your period coming, it's late isn't it. I said, "No not really, sometimes it might be a little late, but it'll be here."

I thought Mike would be happy about a baby, but I'm not sure. Being pregnant might make him feel as though the pressure is on to move into our own place sooner. Now I'd have to find the right time to tell him.

After Rob and Sherrie had visited us several times they decided they like this area. Rob and his wife were looking for a change, and this might be it. Guess what, they now lived two houses from us. Sherrie and I became like sisters, Rob was okay, but my family and I took to Sherrie instantly.

Junie ....
I was still dating around, you know, taking my time. I enjoying myself, but I know I hope to get married and settle down one day, but I wasn't out there pushing for it. When it happened it happened. I saw too many people get married for the wrong reasons and it was a mess. They were miserable and sticking it out through the misery or they'd just throwing in the towel. When I do get married I'm truly going to try to make it work forever, so I had to try to make sure it's the right one.
I had my Grandmother on my mind a lot today, I was missing her and thinking about some of the things she used to tell me. Grandma always gave good advice.

Marie..............
Today was the day I had got to tell this man I was pregnant. Sometimes it's harder than you'd think to tell your man this. Why I don't know, heck I didn't do this by myself, it took both of us.

I told Aunt Kate I wanted to prepare a romantic dinner for Mike and I tonight, so I needed the house to myself from five until about eight this evening, and to tell Grandpa. They were like that's no problem, and they were off and gone. Anyway, when Mike got home,

I was smelling even better than the dinner I had fixed for him. He walked over and gave me a kiss. "Go take your shower sweetheart, dinner and I will be on the table when you come down."

"What's this all about," he asked?

"Just go take your shower, you'll find out what this is all about when you come back down here and don't keep me waiting," I called as he went up the stairs. I could hear him fumbling around in the bedroom, so I lit a few candles and just about closed the shades and blinds to dim the room. He came back down shirtless, he had his shirt on his arm. All I could think to myself is, him looking like that is what got me like this. I was putting our plates on the table, while he was rubbing my butt, and telling me, "That sure does look good, this is real nice."

Mike pulled my chair out for me, then seated himself across from me. We were talking about a little of everything, but I still hadn't brought up this bundle I'm carrying. Dinner was delicious, conversation was good and all, but I still hadn't done it. Finally I decided to clean up the kitchen, it was sweet that Mike offered his help and of course I accepted. I was washing dishes and he was coming in from putting out the trash and I was just like, "Mike, I don't know how you're going to take this-but I'm pregnant."

He just stood there for a second, then he said, "Are you sure?"

"Yes, I'm sure, are you mad?"

"No, I'm just a little surprised, but I'm happy as hell", he said.

He walked over and gave me a hug that said it all. I could finally breathe a sigh of relief.

The next day we told everybody we could think of about us having a baby on the way.

I swear I was getting bigger by the day, stomach just growing and getting a little extra butt and breasts too.

Mike was glad of the breasts growing, to be honest so was I. I wished they'd stay this size.

Carrying this baby was starting to take a toll on me, I guess I needed a little more rest then I normally did. So it was a Thursday night, around eight-thirty p.m., and I was in the bed watching television I woke up, Mike wasn't home. He was out more often then he used to be, with the boys, or working out. Then it was twelve-thirty a.m., when I heard the door open and Mike come in.

"You asleep," Mike asked?

"Not anymore, where have you been? You should have called, I could have needed you to bring something home or I just might needed you to come home," I said.

"Need me to come home for what," he asked?

"Because you're my husband and because I'm pregnant and I just may have needed some help with something or may not have been feeling too good," I told him.

"Yeah, okay, if I don't come straight home, I'll call," Mike said.

"At least," is all I could say.

Friday he came home and brought dinner with him, and I was glad because I didn't feel like cooking when I got home from work. This coming Friday would be my last day of work. Saturday came and damned near went and I hadn't seen much of him, not until around two a.m., when he came strolling in, from hanging out.

"Look Mike, I'm feeling you're out too much, I understand everybody needs some time to themselves, but you're not by yourself. "

"You're right pretty girl, I'm just having a little trouble dealing with me becoming a father. I'm glad-don't get me wrong, just life is happenin' so fast, you know," he said.

I'm telling you things got a little better while I was pregnant, but it wasn't what I was expecting. The doctor said I was due in February, so now it's February and I'm having pains in my back and stomach. I figured I'd better call Momma.

"Momma I'm having pains in my back and stomach, do you think I'm in labor," I asked in between pains.

"Yeah, baby I think so, how far apart are the pains," Momma asked.

"Oh I'd say maybe fifteen minutes apart, I'd better go to the hospital I think," I whined.

"Get your stuff together, is Mike there? Okay, good, tell him to take you to the hospital now. Be very careful, it's a blizzard out there, it's snowing so hard you can't even see, and it must already be a foot and a half deep. Me and your Daddy will meet you there. Be careful, not to fall and not to have an accident," Momma said.

"Mike let's go to the hospital, I'm in labor. Your baby is ready," I said as calm as I could.

He jumped up in a panic, ran to the bedroom grabbed my bag, got my coat, and his keys, and he helped me to the car through mounds of snow. I could see for myself how hard the snow was coming down, Momma was right to emphasize being careful. We had no other choice but to creep along. "This is like driving through milk," Mike said.

Finally, we made it to the hospital. Lord, about nine hours later, our daughter was born. Mike's face was full of tears, seeing him like this made feel such a deep love for him.

Three days later our baby and I went home, Mike picked us up from the hospital. The ground was still covered with mounds of snow. Mike helped me to the car, then went back to get the baby from the nurse, and off we went to my parents house to show everybody the baby, again. Everybody had seen her except Taz, she was so excited, to see the baby. Of course, she wanted to hold Monica, but we didn't think that was a good idea, but she was so intent looking and touching her, I said, "If you sit here on the sofa, sit all the way back, and I'll let you hold the baby."

She sat right down, and I placed my baby in her little arms. Taz was only four years old, but letting her hold the baby made her day. A little while later we went home to my Grandfather's house, where we lived. Grandpa and Aunt Kate were waiting, they held the little bundle and then Aunt Kate told me to go upstairs and lay down, by this time my momma and Taz walked in the door. Momma, Aunt Kate and I went upstairs so they could get me and the baby settled in and comfortable. I didn't know it then, but two hours later when I woke up, I realized they were right, I had been more exhausted than I realized.

I got up looked out the window, to see, you guessed it, more snow falling.

When I went down the stairs my Grandpa was watching Monica sleep. Mike made me a delicious sandwich to hold me over until dinner. The phone rang, since I was the closest to it, I answered. It was a cousin calling to see how we were doing and to say some of them would be by tomorrow to see us. And they did, the next day we had quite a few visitors, none of them stayed too long, so we could get some rest in between the next group of visitors that would be coming by soon.

Three months later..........

I hated to leave my Grandpa's house, but Mike and I moved to our little bungalow. It was cute and cozy. Taz said it reminded her of where the three bears lived. We had a large bedroom, enough room to put the baby's things in our bedroom without being cramped, another smaller bedroom that we'd move Monica to in a few months, a pretty large kitchen where we put our kitchen set, a nice sized pantry and a living room, and porch. I was hoping this ass would act better then he had been.

When our baby turned two years old, I planned to get a job, even if it was part-time, that'll get me out the house and add a little money to our pockets. Mike insisted no, I should stay home with Monica. He was probably right on that part. I didn't admit it to him though, just in case I had to get a job earlier than two years from now.

For now we were the happy little family at least for this week, now let's hope it stayed this way. Mike was home most of the time and really helpful with everything. As my little sister said, we're like the three bears in our little cave here.

As time went on, Mike started spending less time home, again. I spoke with him about it a few times, and things got better for a few days, then he went back to coming in all times of the morning.

This one day my Mother and Taz were over visiting me and Monica, we hardly had any food, so my Mother and Taz went to the corner store to get some food for us, mainly for my baby. She had started eating baby food, and she loved mashed potatoes, so I gave her mashed potatoes often. Anyway, my mother and sister were at the corner store, and Taz saw my husband in the store with some white woman hanging on him, she tapped my mother and told her to look over there, "There's Mike with that woman," she said to Momma. My mother went over to them and told him, "I'm here at this store buying food, because your baby is home hungry, you son of a bitch". Then she told the white woman she better leave him alone, before somebody beat her ass. The white chick didn't say a word she stepped back like she was somewhat surprised and scared.

Mike didn't say anything to my mother, she'd have put it on him if he'd talked trash to her. Momma and Taz came right back with some food and told me what had gone on at the store. Mike didn't come right behind them, he must have taken that bitch home first. About thirty-five minutes later he came home, as soon as he stepped foot in the door I demanded to know, "What the fuck were you doing with that woman? Oh, she must have been helping you carry food to your car so you could bring it home to your baby."

I had just laid Monica on the bed, when that fool grabbed me by my hair and started fighting me, like I'd done something wrong. It was on, he was strong as a bull, but I was giving it my all to get free, when my mother jumped in and got him off me. That's when I grabbed the iron and started swinging it to kill. I guess he figured this fool is crazy , so without saying anything he left. I went to the bathroom to get myself together, and my little sister came in to see if I needed any help and if I was okay. Monica was crying, so my mother had picked the baby up and quieted her down. They stayed another couple of hours keeping me company and not believing what had just happened. My mother wasn't too surprised she had been threw the dirt and mud with my father and had seen it all, she said. Taz was in the room with the baby watching television while Momma and I talked, she told me she couldn't tell me what to do, whatever I did she was behind me, but not to tolerate the shit she had tolerated.

"We're fine Momma, ya'll go home and we'll be okay, he won't come back here tonight."

"Get whatever you'll need for tomorrow and come on home," Momma told me.

"No that's okay, I'll be over in the morning. I'll be ready at nine."

After they left, I got ready for bed, and the pistol he kept hidden, I made sure it was loaded and laid it under the edge of the pillow next to me. If he wanted to start some more shit, I'd be the one to end the shit. I wasn't going to take no ass whippings or take a chance at him trying to kill me.

As I laid in the bed trying to relax, the doorbell rang. I asked who was at the door, it was my mother, I opened the door.

"Marie, I'm not gonna leave here unless you and Monica come with us, now get whatever you'll need to take with you," Momma said.

She convinced me, so I got some things together for the both of us and off we went for the night.

When we got home, my Poppa was watching television.

"What's going on, baby," Poppa asked?

"Me and Mike had an argument, so I came here for the night."

"You and the baby alright", he asked?

"Yeah, Poppa we're fine, I'll watch television with you for a while. Let me put Monica down so she can get some rest, then I'll be right back," I told Poppa.

Momma had sat down on the sofa, Poppa was looking at her with a question in his eyes. Like what went on over there? Momma left as I had told him, we'd just had an argument. Poppa knew it must have been a big argument for me to come home. I put the baby in the living room, then went to the kitchen. From the kitchen I asked if anybody wanted anything, while I was there. Poppa and I had a beer and Momma had a soda, while we watched television.

I went to bed, in my old bedroom, Taz squeezed in with me.

The next afternoon Allen came to talk me and of course asked what was the deal. I told him most of what had happened, because I know how protective my brother was, I knew if I told him everything, he'd kill Mike. I didn't want any trouble, but Allen was good at reading people. He didn't tell me he was going to kick his ass, he said he was going to speak to Mike about this and he got up off the sofa, I grabbed his elbow and said, "Don't start any mess with him, it's not worth it. I can handle it." Allen said I'm just going to talk to him and went out to his car to go find Mike.

I knew he was going to tell Junie what had happened, between the two of them this could become extremely ugly. We always believed in not getting involved in somebody else's affairs, because you could end up being the outsider, the couple will probably get back together and they'll both be mad at you for messing in their business, but I guess this was different, having some nigger running around, not providing for his family and then going to fight me.

I put some music on the hi-fi, and went back into the kitchen. Me, Momma, Taz, Paula, and Aunt Kate were in the kitchen when Allen came in the back door. I could look at him and tell something had gone on. I didn't ask him anything, I just looked in his eyes with a question. Allen said he'd gone to talk to Mike.

"What happened", I asked?

"I asked the dude what the hell is the problem over here. He said for me to mind my business. I stepped a little closer to him, and said you fucking over my sister is my business. Like I said, what's the deal", I asked him.

"He told me his side of the story, shady you know. Then I told him I didn't appreciate what went down, and asked him would he be able to correct what's going on. If not to let Marie know so, then he pushed me aside and I swung on him. We threw a punch, then the dude from the front house came running off his back porch to stop us, but we had already stopped. I didn't have intentions of fighting, although I knew it might come to that, but something had to be done. I told him, this is not a threat, it's a promise, that if he touched you again, I'd whipped his ass for sure, and that was that", Allen told us.

"Marie, don't run back today, take your time and think about things first", Aunt Kate told me. Aunt Kate was the most laid back person until you made her mad, if it had been her fighting with her husband, she'd have won the fight for sure. She would have laid his ass down, like she'd done before.

Later that day Mike came to see me at my parents', he apologized and told me what happened with him and Allen. He said he wasn't mad at him, he had to respect him for confronting him about the situation. Also, Junie came to see him at the gym about our situation, he made it clear it wouldn't be tolerated. I was thinking to myself, in order for him to stay friendly with the rest of the men in the family, they shouldn't hear about this. So that night I went back to our little house,
I told Mike to go on, my Momma would bring Monica and I home later.

Junie came in from work and gave everybody a kiss. Papa came in about ten minutes after him. The guys went in the den to relax for a while before dinner.

I went on home later that night Momma, Taz, and Aunt Kate dropped me off. Mike was there on the sofa watching and sleeping over television. "Allen told me he came by here. I asked him not to", I told Mike.
"Yeah, he and Junie came by and promised to beat my ass or kill me if this happened again. Believe me I'm not scared of them, but I was wrong, I can't be mad at you or them. I don't know where my head was", Mike said.
"I apologize, but it doesn't begin to make up for what I've done. Just please try to give me a chance to make it

up, it won't happen again. I promise", he said sounding so sad.

"Don't forget about Allen's going away party", I told him.

"I won't forget, ya'll need me to do anything," he asked?

"It's pretty much all taken care of, it's next Tuesday at seven," I reminded him.

Insert?

Allen..........

I was telling Junie that Trina had left for Virginia this morning and how I really had a good time with her and she had a great sense of humor. She had planned on going back to Virginia, before being sent to her new post in Texas. This coming Friday I was driving to Virginia to see Trina before she left for Texas. Coffee and cream, she was everything wrapped in one package.

Trina and I had a great weekend together, she also introduced me to her Grandparents. Late Sunday afternoon, I returned from visiting Trina, time was going by too fast. I figured I should get a start on getting some things together to take with me when I left for basic training. This shit was scary, more than likely I'll end up in Vietnam. I mean literally in Vietnam fighting for my country. More importantly, is that I'll be fighting for my life and my sanity. Man, my cousin Dave had already gone, he was in North Carolina. Junie had come back from Nam last year, the Air Force didn't keep him because of a high school knee injury. His knee had been crushed playing in a basketball game, the doctors rebuilt his knee, it was held together with pins, bolts, and screws. They said Junie would walk with a severe limp, but he fooled them. He regained full used of his leg and knee, continued being an athlete and had no limp at all.

The only good thing that might come out of this military thing, was Trina being in Texas so I'd get to see her again.

As the days past by I thought of something my father used to say to us when we were small, "Set over there and let me look at you for a while". Now he and I were both looking at each other, whether we're setting around or moving about, I'd catch him watching me and vice versa. I'm going to miss my family, you know we're close. My Mother's planning a going away party for me, I swear she's the best mother in the world.

Marie..............
The evening of the party people started coming early, which was good, because there's always a few last minute things you need done.
Everybody was having a good, yet sad time. There was plenty of dancing, hugging, laughing eating, drinking and reminiscing about every event that ever happened, some even had written some poetry for my brother's going away. To be honest before the night was over there was quite a bit of tears running too, and yes I was one of the teary face people.

This is something that we weren't able to avoid, I wasn't trying to hide it from anybody, I was scared as hell. Scared when Junie went to war and so relieved when he came back to us and very blessed he came back in the same shape he left in. Now, my baby brother's going to Vietnam, all I can do is pray and you can believe the Lord knows it's me and he knows what I'm going to talk about as usual.

Allen..............

Just like my high school graduation party, my going away party was a blast, there were a lot of people there, family came from out of state, and seemed like half the county was at my party.

It had come that time for me. I was about to leave for basic training. I had been keeping Trina posted on what was going on here, so she'd know about when to expect me. I was praying Lord, let me make it back home safe. My parents, Aunt Kate and little sister were taking me to Newark airport, that's were I was to meet the officer from the Air Force, along with other draftees.

So the day was actually here, and we headed to the airport. Taz was watching me like a hawk, she was taking in every move I made, making a mental note of every detail about me. I could see it in her little eyes and the yearning for me not to go, but I told her I have to go, but I'll be back. She believed me, but it hurt me to see, a little girl so affected by what was going on around her and understanding it. So we're setting around this one section where all the guys were to line up when this guy comes to put us on the plane, I met this cool white boy, whose was looking through his bag to make sure he wasn't forgotten his straightening comb. I was like - what? He said, "Yeah man, I have to use it to make this stuff lay down like this, slick you know."

Finally, we had to line up to leave and the family was crying, but I had to continue to be strong or at least put on the strong front. We exchanged our hugs and kisses so long, that when I returned back to my assigned group they were lined up to board, at this point I couldn't look back at my family now. I had to just go on, I knew if I looked back, then I'd be a mess.

By the time we actually arrived at the fort it was the next day. The military won't take you directly to where they want you to be, they have to take you everywhere else and then there, I guess for security reasons. It was hot as hell down here in Texas, and as soon as I got a chance I had to write home. Next on my mind was when am I going to get to see Trina.

And so my journey began, training was hard, challenging, and kind of funny at the end of the day when it was over. The guys and I would sit back and laugh at some of the stupid things we'd have done all day, or answer letters from loved ones. I got quite a bit of mail from Junie, Marie, Taz, and Trina. My parents didn't write me, they just added whatever they want to say to the letters from the rest of the family. I talked to them when I got to call home. As the weeks went by I realized I may have changed some, I seemed so serious or stern at times. I guess they called it being a soldier, some called it learning to be a killing machine, as for me I called it doing what it takes to survive.

This weekend I was on leave, so I be spent it with Coffee and Cream, in Waco. Just a quiet weekend, okay a little clubbing on Friday, then it was romance all the way.

About two more weeks would pass before I was shipped off. Where you want to know? I wanted to know too, they don't tell you much of anything until the last minute, and then things will probably change while you're in transit. Until that time I planned to spend every free minute with Trina.

Finally, another chance to see Coffee and Cream, and to explore some of the area, a group of us went to San Antonio, this place was beautiful with history. Trina knew lots of nice spots, so we went wherever she recommended. First, we went to a Mexican spot for dinner, and then to some little club for a drink and a dancing. After a little dancing our group began to break up, going off to do their own thing. Remember, I mentioned romance that previous weekend, well this night would be a repeat performance. After dinner and dancing we got a nice little room and some drinks to take back to our room, Trina didn't drink so we got some soda also. She went in the bathroom to freshen herself up, she was fresh enough for me, but when she came out, she had on this sexy two piece set, it was a burgundy color trimmed in lace. I emphasize, she made it look good. I couldn't wait for her to get to the bed where I was waiting, I got up and went to her standing at the bathroom door. First I kissed her on her chest, not breasts, her chest then down to her breasts, I kissed her arms, neck and finally her lips. Her legs were smooth they looked like she had on stockings. I escorted her to the bed and we set on the side while I poured us a drink of our choice, then I leaned her back and ran my hands up and down her legs, across her hips, stomach, breasts, then back down and stopped when I reached her crotch. Man, I was so excited I could have burst, but some how I held myself together and tried to be cool. I'll let your imagination fill in the rest of what happened, I don't kiss and tell.

I spent more time with Trina again before I left Texas, and we talked every night.

Now this shit was getting thick, we're going to the real deal. One of the dudes traveling was all teared up, because he's hoping he makes it back to his wife and baby. For the most part the flight was pretty quiet. Just waiting for whatever is coming next, praying to make it out of this shit alive and sane, and if by chance I'm to die, just let it be so quick I don't know what happened.

Where my group ended up being stationed wasn't as bad as we expected, we weren't in a combat zone. The Air Force is not put directly in the middle of action most times, the native people there treated us pretty decent.

It had been about three weeks since I gotten here and I had just gotten letters from Trina, and from home since I had gotten here. Things at home were fine, everybody's hanging in there, Trina was telling me she's pregnant. When I wrote back I asked her what did she want to do, get married, or have an abortion. I then told her how much I truly didn't want her to have an abortion, and if it was up to me we'd get married, but I'd leave it up to her to let me know what she wanted to do, and if she would be getting out of the Army. I also let them know back home she was pregnant and if we had to, could she come to live with them until I got home. My family said yes to my asking if she could live with them until I got home, to be honest I knew they would say yes. Trina responded to my letter saying yes, she'd finished her time and is getting out of the Army and no she wasn't having an abortion. The marriage part she left me hanging on. So I then wrote and told her, my family was waiting for her to come live with them, until I got home. I also told her that by the time she received this letter I will have spoken with her.

We wrote each other back and forth for a few weeks, before I was able to call the states to speak with everyone.

I called home first to talk with my parents to update them on all that was happening, they were happy for Trina to come live with them, they'd take good care of her and our baby until I arrived home.

Then I called to speak with my sweetheart, this was something we needed to discuss, not write each other about. She was happy to go to my parents' house, so this would make things easier for us. I felt if she had gone home to her family, she and people would doubt my feelings for her, and didn't want that.

Junie............

Allen called to tell us Trina would be arriving in two weeks. The next day Trina called and told us she'd see us in a few weeks.

It was a Thursday evening, when Trina arrived by train, but she didn't call to have anybody pick her up from the train station, she took a cab to the house. Trina said there was too much snow to have someone come pick her up.When she got inside, we realized how big she was, by that I mean she was carrying a lot of baby in her stomach. Mom and myself went out to get her things from the cab. The cab driver starting telling us Trina had fallen off the train. Trina said she hadn't gotten hurt and that she was okay. Taz was checking her out big time, like so she's going to be here waiting for my brother, I hope she's not going to be a pest. Trina wasn't a pest though, she was a very nice girl, smart, pretty, and helpful around the house. She even got Taz to clean under her bed, by telling her if she didn't clean under her bed those dust balls under there would turn into people, bad people. I'd never seen a little girl clean with such determination in my life. Trina blended right in with the family. Some people actually thought she resembled my Mom they had green and hazel eyes.

One day Trina was making a strawberry short cake, Taz told her," I don't like strawberries". "Have you ever had them before", Trina asked?
"No" Taz answered.
"How can you not like something you've never even tried before", while handing Taz a strawberry, "How's that," Trina asked?
Taz, said back, "That was good."
"See, I thought you'd like it. Have another one, then get the sugar so we can sweeten them just right for desert tonight."

Taz fell right in with her, they shared the bedroom my brother and I used to share, I moved into the bedroom that was once Marie's.

The holiday season had arrived; I love this time of year, although I thrive on the ocean and the beach. Anyway, it was a week before Christmas when my brother Allen came home. Man, we celebrated, just the two of us, then with family, but the whole time the wedding was also being planned for Trina and Allen.

Just picture this, it's Christmas Eve night and it's snowing, we already had about ten inches on the ground. That night in the church it was a little dim, with candle lights lit all along the window panes Mom, Dad, Taz, Marie, Mike, Grandpa, Aunt Kate, and I were there at the church my siblings and myself had grown up in. As Allen and Trina were saying their vows, Allen was nervous and when it was time for him to repeat after the preacher, he started laughing, and laughing, and trying to repeat after the preacher, and laughing. I was standing next to him and I knew he was laughing because he was so nervous, so I kept telling him to come on and stop all this laughing. Mean while, poor Trina was looking at him like what in the hell is wrong, is this a damned joke. Finally, he got the words out. Even with all his laughter, it was still a beautiful event. Afterwards we were getting back in the cars, snow began falling so hard we could barely see in front of us. Threw all the blowing snowflakes falling from the night sky we made it back to my parents' house where we had a small reception with a wedding cake big enough for thirty people.

Damn, two married. Will I be next? I'm in no hurry for that, I gots to be sure, or at least think I'm really really sure.

Allen...........

Hey man, we did it, tied the knot. It was awful not being able to stop laughing at the alter, I felt so bad for Trina, because I was thinking she's got to be offended or my laughing had to be hurting her feelings. She was looking at me like what the hell?

We continued staying with my parents for a few more weeks. From here we moved to an apartment house owned by some people we knew. Actually we'd be living next to my Uncle C. The apartment was an attic apartment, it's a real good size apartment, two bedrooms, kitchen, dining area, and a huge living room. The only thing I would have a problem with were those slanted ceilings and walls. If I wasn't careful I could knock my damned head off with one false move.

Man, it's the middle of January already and Trina's stomach had gotten so big, now she's telling me we can't have sex, it's too uncomfortable. She ate ice and ground her teeth half the night, she had no control over these food cravings, I thought, I'll be damned glad when the baby gets here, no sex and running out getting her Chinese food day and night.

"Trina, I'm going to the store for a minute. You want anything other than ice", I asked her.

"No funny man, I can't think of anything right off hand. Maybe some Chinese food", she answered as I picked up keys from the coffee table.

Alright, be back", I told her.

Let's see, I was thinking as I walked to the car, she has about two more months to go.

As I looked up at the sky, it looked like it was gonna snow again. I got in the car and backed out the driveway and off I went. I made it to the store, before the snow started, but by the time I got to the Chinese restaurant, the snow started to fall. Falling by the buckets,

I rushed in to place my order, so I can get back home to snuggle in our little nest, oh yeah and not have sex.

As I walk in the doorway, she had lit some candles and was in the bed watching television, waiting for my return or the Chinese food. She told me, her and my mother had gone next door to my Uncle C's house earlier today. Trina and my Uncle C's daughter Gloria had gotten pretty close, they hang around together alot.

She came in the kitchen to help me carry everything back to the bedroom, where we stayed for the rest of the night, except for one trip she made to get more ice.

My brother had been saying it would be awhile until he got married he wanted to make sure what he was doing was the right thing. It was the second week of January, and listen to this, Junie's and Paula's wedding was just a few days off, I was the best man and Trina was the maid of honor. Neither one of us had a bachelor party, why I don't know. Some of us guys got together two days before Junie's wedding and went to New York to party, then the night before his wedding us guys went to a local bar to drink and talk and maybe see a few strippers. Man, we got our heads bad, I don't remember how we even got home. Their day came and Junie and Paula got married right there at my parent's house, nobody in attendance except the immediate family and the preacher.

The weeks are passing, getting close to the end of Trina's pregnancy; my family and I keep a close check on her, even through the day, when we were at work. We were working on getting the nursery ready and the next thing we knew, March rolled around and this baby was ready to check us out. As Trina told me she was ready to go to the hospital, I remained calm. I called my Mother to tell her we were going to the hospital, then I got Trina and her bag then off we went to the military hospital. Thank

God, there was no snow on the ground, because it's not
the closest hospital, but we made it there just fine.
A little while later, they came and told me we'd had a
boy, a beautiful, healthy baby boy. Man, my face was wet
with tears of joy. I went to see my family, they both were
beautiful, as I held him I couldn't even speak, all I could
do was look at him in awe. Trina said, "We said we'd
name him after you."
All I could do was kiss her and look at him some more.

A few days later my wife and baby came home,
my Mom, Aunt Kate, and Marie had come over and had
the place picture perfect waiting for them. They'd done
enough shopping to last at least a month, food, baby
goods, clothes and household needs.
My little sister came over almost every day already, but
now when she came to see us, she was very attentive to
the baby and very good with him. Trina could do her
work or rest while Taz was here. She was too short to
reach in the playpen to get little Allen out, but everything
else, she had covered.

Little Allen was five weeks old, when my
Grandfather past away. I was so glad Grandpa saw his
first great grandson. Here we go again, losing someone
so significant to our family, a part of us. Again family and
friends came from all over the place for my Grandfather's
funeral. My Grandpa had been a farmer in North Carolina
and a landscaper here in New Jersey. Everybody came,
he was such an honorable man, that loved what he did
for a living, Grandpa loved watching and helping plants
and flowers grow. His yard had always had animals and
plenty of fruits, vegetables and flowers. He handed that
trait down to his family. I enjoy seeing pretty flowers and
I like animals, I just don't take part in raising them or
hunting them.

After Little Allen turned one, we decided to get him a puppy. It was a cute little German Shepard that liked to bite my toes for some reason. Trina said he bit my feet because they stank. No he didn't bite anybody else's feet, just mine, maybe she was right about my feet. Some days I'd come home sit back on the sofa, take off my shoes, put my feet up to relax and here he'd come to greet me. Then before you know it, he'd be nipping on my toes, getting on my damned nerves.

I told Trina, "Look Trina, if this mutt doesn't stop biting me, I'm gonna get rid of him."

Trina said, laughing at this dog working so hard to get my feet, "Really, I don't understand it, he's crazy over your toes. They must smell like food to him. They don't smell like anything I'd like to put in my mouth, but maybe he'll grow out of it. It's so funny looking at the two of you going at it though."

I grabbed that damned crazy dog and found some rope and tied him to the living room door, to keep him away from me. The nut probably didn't mean any harm, but those little teeth were sharp. There were times we'd have him tied to a bicycle outside and when the mailman came the puppy would chase him down the driveway dragging the tricycle behind him.

I'd say another five or six weeks past and this puppy was still giving my toes hell. I'd come in from work do my same routine, started getting into Star Trek and next thing you know, that puppy had my big toe. "Look, this crazy dog's outta here. Pack his stuff, I'm gonna find another home for him."

We ended up giving him to some people we knew and as the puppy grew older he grew meaner and meaner.

Junie............

I had dated quite a few beauties, straight up beauties. I was being real with Paula, but there were still a few women still giving Paula and I trouble, no matter how I tried to get them out the way.

One day Paula and I had gone to Two Guys a department store and just happened to run into a pain in the ass that lived across the street from me. This girl had been chasing me, and my brother for years, since early high school. Somehow I let trouble happen in the store right in front of Paula. Kathy was fine and she knew it, she kept throwing herself at me right in front of Paula. I guess I wasn't putting my foot down firm enough right then. So when Paula and I got back to the car, she was fuming and fussing. I was already agitated at the show that had just gone on with Kathy and I'm mad because Paula's in my face. She kept fussing at me and the next thing I knew I had smushed her in the face pushing her back out of my face. Man, before I could apologize to her, she told me, "I wouldn't tolerate being disrespected and especially not in public. I have a car and my own money and I work every day. I mean it Junie, I won't take that shit." Paula was right, I should have controlled the situation better and now I felt like shit after letting the situation get out of hand. I could tell she wasn't just talking or threatening me, she meant every word she said and I respected her for that. Believe me I would never put my hand on her again.

Guess what, it was close to a year and Paula and I are still hanging in there, after all the drama I had brought to the table with me, the chick showing out in the store, another one always riding by my house and the night she threw yellow paint on my new black sport car. Maybe I didn't bring the drama come to think of it, maybe the drama was chasing me. Paula and I were talking about old times and our parent's reaction to us dating. My Dad didn't say anything about me dating a white girl, he'd keep his opinion to himself and just sit back and watch. My Mother on the other hand, was different; if it was on her mind, you were going to hear it, more than once. Mom's reaction to me dating a white girl had been, "Junie let me see you in the kitchen for a minute." I went in the kitchen, and she told me, "Get that white girl out of my house." Now they get along like mother and daughter, they really love each other. My mother and Paula do almost everything together, Paula is always at the house, or with Trina and Marie.

Paula didn't have much of a choice, but to be around all the time. Her parents disowned her, for being with me. She got a room at the hospital where we worked, and I helped her move her things in, she didn't have much to move, because anything they'd given her, her mother had taken back. I told her this is a huge step she had taken. She had told me I was everything to her, my family made her feel more loved and welcomed than she'd ever felt in anybody's home and she'd been to quite a few homes, both adoption homes and foster homes. Rumor had it, her birth father had her mother killed because he thought she was cheating on him, everybody said there was no way she would have done anything like that, she truly loved her husband and family. After having his wife killed, he put the three children in an adoption home. While growing up Paula, her brother and sister had been separated and lost track of each other.

We finished fixing her new room up and went out for a bite to eat, but she wanted to go to my house. "Maybe your Mother or Father will have cooked," Paula said. She had no sound of regret in her voice, I looked at her with those big brown eyes and gave her a warm kiss of reassurance. Off we sped down Highway 34 making it to check my Mom's kitchen. Right on time as usual, was still hot. My family had just started eating, Paula got a plate from the cabinet to fix her plate of food (smothered pork chops, mashed potatoes, biscuits, and turnip greens) and sat at the table with them.

"Hey there, how's everybody," Allen said walking in the door as everybody except my father was leaving the table, Allen and I went in the living room, while the women took a bag of candies and went on the front porch .

Uncle Rob, came in the front door, "What's for dinner," he asked.

I replied, "Help yourself dinner's on the stove."

"I don't want anything, just stopped in to see how everybody's doin'. Mattie told me she was over earlier today. Perry how's your tomatoes comin" along?"

Pops answered, "Man, something is having a field day in my garden, I sprayed for bugs, but I think it might be rabbits or groundhogs."

"Well, I'm gonna go home, but come on over if you get a chance, he said to my father. "See everybody later."

" Take some gravy and biscuits and I'll walk over with you, and see what's going on with your garden", Dad told Uncle Rob.

"I might as well get a taste," Uncle Rob said.

My Uncle Rob lived in the house behind ours.

Allen had gone home to his wife and baby, we had eaten dinner and it was about an hour later when, Aunt Kate, and Taz and I went to visit Uncle Rob. Mom said she'd stay home and enjoy the quiet while we were gone. Our house wasn't noisy, but it usually busy.

Two months later

Marie............

Mike, Monica and I had moved to south Jersey with his family. It was a small house, but somehow we all fit in there. His family farmed for a living, we lived on a road with no other houses, just fields and fields of vegetables mostly corn.

Let me tell you, when the weekend came, the house turned into Las Vegas, card games and gambling all weekend long, twenty-four hours a day. It was just the family playing, but I had never seen people love cards like this. All weekend they played, day and night. I couldn't complain, I was pretty happy there, his family was so good to me and Monica, I just missed my family. There was a remedy for that too though. My Mom, Dad and Taz came to visit me often, then some weekends when we'd visit my parents also.

Some times they'd move their card-a-thon, we'd all pack up and go to my parents house and to their son Robby and his wife, that live right down the street from my family.

Time was passing on and I was still having a problem with Mike being away from home too much for my taste. This night I was setting around here playing it cool, waiting for this nigger to get in so I can set his ass straight. You know I'm not the type to complain and nag just for the hell of it, but even his family had mentioned his being out too much to both myself and to him.

They were still playing cards and drinking, Monica had been put to bed, Rochelle, Mike's younger sister and I were watching television and I was silently counting the hours waiting for Mike to come in.

Mike came strolling in like it's two o'clock in the afternoon, instead of two in the morning. "Where've you been" I asked?

"At the gym, I know it's late", he said.

"That's a damned lie", I said.

"What's your problem", he said.

"You're the problem, but not for long, if you keep this shit up", I told him.

"What you mean, not for long", Mike said.

"Just what I said, don't try me", I told him.

"Look watch your mouth, Marie."

"While I watch my mouth, you'd better watch everything you do, I've really about had enough of this shit", I said.

He just walked away like he was too tired to fuss. I didn't want to fuss any way, if he'd stop this shit, I wouldn't have to get like this.

I got in the bed while Mike was in the shower, when he came to bed he had nothing to say and believe me neither did I.

The following week went on as normal, some days he came on time and the others, usually the weekend he'd come in whenever.

"Mike look, you're not here that much and basically you're not doing too great supporting us anyway. So I don't be a burden to your family or to you or slow you from hanging out until who knows when, I'm gonna be leaving here, this coming Friday."

"Marie stop talking stupid, you're not going anywhere and especially not with my daughter", Mike said.

"If you say so Mike, I guess I'll keep trying to hang in there", I told him in a sarcastic way, just to shut his mouth.

"Look, I'm going to bed," I told him.

While coming upstairs behind me he touched the back of my leg, I wanted to kick him in his face, yet somehow I controlled myself.

Mike got in the bed, trying to talk sweet, just talking about his day, and asking what had Monica and I been up to all day. "To be honest I'm not in the mood to talk, I'm sleepy", I told him.

"Okay we'll talk and spend the day together tomorrow, even if it's Tuesday, I'll take the day off. How does that sound", he asked?
"That sounds good", I told him.
I was drifting off to sleep when I felt him pull his hard muscular body up against my back and I do mean his hard body. He felt good, even though I was upset and disappointed at how things were going. I didn't react to his body like I used to would have done. I ignored him and I drifted off to sleep.
Mike took the day off and we went into town for lunch, then we went to the park, Monica loved the little swings and things that were there. Later around
six thirty just he and I went out for dinner with his brother and his wife.
I did enjoy dinner, because I liked his brother and his wife and I had become very good friends.

To be honest when we got home I was pretty tired and so was he. Mike's sister had babysat Monica, Monica had already been put to bed, so I showered and headed for bed to watch television and sleep. Mike came in about an hour later he rubbed my behind, thigh, breasts, and started rubbing my love mound. It felt good, even though I didn't want it to. I tried to ignore his touching me there, so I rubbed his arm. I guess as a distraction. Well it wasn't working too well, I wanted to have sex with him, not make love as I did before. So I spread my legs some so he could really caress me there, I licked his nipples and rubbed his erect manhood. I have to admit he was fine as hell, and a pain in the ass. So he got on top of me and he entered my good wet stuff. The sex was good as usual, but after it was over, I was kind of empty of feelings, just sexually satisfied. I almost wanted to cry because of the way I was feeling or my lack of feelings. I was still leaving his ass the end of this week.

Thursday night around six that evening my folks pulled up, Momma, Allen, Aunt Kate, and Taz. I was all packed and ready to leave. The only things I had were some clothes for me and my baby. They came in and talked to Mike's family for a few minutes. His family understood what I was doing and why. You know we said our good-byes and kissed and they told us they'd still be coming to visit us. You know how people say things, they don't mean any harm or to lie, but I guess it just seems the right thing to say at that time. We left the little farmhouse and headed back for home.

Well as time past, low and behold, they did come to see us. A few times out of the year I went to visit them also, I stayed at my ex-sister in-laws place, she had left her husband and moved back home to south Jersey.

It had been a year, since I left Mike. I never said it was easy to do or that it was easy to stay away. I still missed him once in a while even though he'd done me wrong.

I was doing hair on the weekends, but it wasn't enough to support Monica and myself. I went on welfare to help out and I was going to beauty culture school. The routine was I'd take a cab or bus to class, then Momma would pick me up afterwards, we'd pick up Monica from the babysitter, sometimes go to the stores then she'd drop Monica and me off at our apartment.

I was thinking about filing for divorce, I was pretty sure by now Mike and I were not getting back together. We had this arrangement for him to pick up Monica from my Aunt's whenever he wanted, he'd have her for Christmas week and two weeks in the summer as long as I wasn't there. That was fine with me, I didn't want to see his black ass anyway. Come to think of it, we were doing better without him.

Anyway life was moving on, tomorrow was Friday and I'd met this fine soldier, no it's not the uniforms that attract me. When I met Donald I had no idea he was in the military, but he asked me out and I gave him my telephone number. He was really a good guy, good to me and to Monica, he was always bringing things for her, a little outfit, a toy, or food. One day he insisted I take some money he was trying to give me, I didn't know how to accept it. You know, you want to take the money and you need to take the money, but you don't want the guy to think of you in a certain way. I guess Donald could see it on my face and he said, "Let me tell you something, I care about you and Monica, I enjoy you and Monica, and I want to be here for the both of you, not just financially. The question is will you let me be here for you. I'd feel bad if you don't let me help out now and then."

He was so sincere when he said these things. Then he said, "I'm going to give Monica a kiss good night", so he went in the bedroom and kissed her. When he returned from her room he gave me a kiss and said, "See you tomorrow"

Monica slept all night and so did I. Saturday morning she woke up to look at her cartoons. When she pulled the covers back to get up, money fell out her bed. "Mommy Mommy, look there's money in my bed", Monica called to me. I went to see what she was talking about. That man had left $80 in her bed. I know you're probably thinking $80, that's not a lot of money, but it was the thought that got me. Also eighty dollars was a lot more cash back in the nineteen-seventies. Hey, and every little bit counts.

I guess it was around four that afternoon when my phone rang and it was Donald, I thanked him. He asked for what, I told him the money. He told me not to thank him for something so small, when I deserved more, as time past he gave more. He had a sharp new corvette convertible, needless to say I couldn't drive, but he insisted he teach me, that way I could use his car when I needed it. After a few attempts to teach me, his nerves and patience gave out. I wasn't that bad of a driver, I just didn't have any real desire to learn. Crazy right? Not driving, but always wanting to go some where. It became usual for him to help us out when he got paid, he'd buy us groceries from the naval post, he got a really good discount there. He was stationed at the naval base close by, so this went on for about two years.

One evening a girlfriend and I went to visit Donald at his place, he wasn't expecting me, but when we arrived I knocked on his door, he opened it without asking who was at the door. When he opened it, he seemed surprised to see me. There was a woman in his living room, she looked like something was going on before I showed up. Donald slid us out the door and asked my girlfriend to excuse us for a minute. He and I walked towards his car, we were arguing a bit, because I could tell he was lying to me about who she was and what she was doing there. He started talking louder, which made me get a tad mad. Now we were at the point of raising hell, he caught me by the upper arm trying to tell me to leave and he'd come over so he and I could talk about this. I snatched my arm away from him, he kept nudging at me in the direction of my girlfriend's car, so I guess to retaliate I picked up a trashcan and threw it through his windshield. He was stunned and frozen still. We were still there going at it, now raising hell about the big ass trash can that had gone clean through his windshield and was laying in the seat of his fine ass car. Some how the police came and asked a few questions, and one of military police said, "Well, you must have done something really wrong to get her so upset she through that clean through your window, that takes a whole lot of strength to do."

The police asked me if I was okay, I answered yes. Then they asked, if I'd like to be escorted to my vehicle, and figured I'd better say yes again, looking at the rage in Donald's eyes. While he stood there frozen my girlfriend Leya ran over and grabbed me so we could get in her car and get away with the help from the police before he got over his shock.

After Leya and I got in her car the two of us rode for a while so I could calm down. She had me laughing at how I had thrown that trash can through his windshield. Then I said to her, he probably will be ready to kill me if he sees me again. I decided before she took me home, that I should leave Monica over my aunt's house tonight, just in case I had to confront him.

Later that evening I walked in my place, feeling upset, and bewildered about earlier today. I had put on some music to cry to, when my doorbell rang, I peeped through the peep hole to see who was there, it was Donald.

I asked through the door, "What do you want?"

"Marie open the door I'm not going to hurt you. We need to clear the air," he answered.

Shit, I wasn't letting this nigger in after what had gone down earlier.

He convinced me to let him inside, and can you believe we talked rationally. I told him maybe we needed to stop seeing each other, because that was out of character for me to have gotten so upset. He didn't try to convince me that wasn't a good idea, he agreed also. So we took a break from seeing each other, after a few weeks past Donald would call me a few times a week just see what was up.

One day Donald asked me to dinner and I accepted his invitation. While we were out he was the gentleman he was before our episode and while we talked over dinner,

I was surprised when Donald asked me to marry him, actually I hadn't gotten divorced yet. He was about to be stationed somewhere else and he said he loved me and didn't want to leave without me, but like an ass I told him no. Well, he went on to San Diego, but kept in touch with me and when he got a chance he came back to see me and ask me again to marry him. I look back and wonder why I didn't marry him. Maybe I was still young and stupid or maybe gun shy, because of my marriage that had gone wrong.

Anyway you can't cry over spilled milk, at least that's how the saying goes. I have to say this man was persistent, because he kept in touch with me and asking me to marry him, then finally he gave up and drifted away.

Now speaking of marriage, guess whose about to jump the broom? You think it might be Junie. Yes, he's about to take the plunge. We thought he was doing the right thing, though. He and Paula got along so well, and she's just very down to earth and sweet. January is the month they chose, so we have four months to get ready for this. They insist they only want the immediate family to attend, something real small.

Allen............

I'd been spending quite a bit of time away from home. Why you wonder, I don't know. It started with me just hanging out with the guys, then the time with them starting growing, some times I'm not with them. Just out, you know?

I do admit I met this girl, we talked for a while that night, I told her I was married. The next time I went to this bar, it was about two or three weeks later, I happened to run into her again. I didn't make any effort to get her attention or start a conversation, I was at the other side of the bar when she saw me, I just gave a hello wave. She came over to speak, so again we said a few words, then the chick bought me a drink and sat down next to me. Normally I find this kind of a turn off, when a chick is the aggressor. Some how she did it kind of in a non-threatening way, not like she was really trying to pick me up.

During our conversation I spoke of my wife and baby, but she just kept talking with me. Before the night was over we danced and I knew her name. She was named Debbi, petite, but a nice little shape on her. I tried to buy her a drink, but she didn't drink alcohol so I bought her a soda. Somewhere in the back of my mind, I could see Trina and our baby what they were probably doing right now and what was probably going on at our home earlier that evening and at the same time the night was getting later and later.

"Look Debbi, it was nice talking with you, but I'd better be heading home," I told her.

"Okay, I understand, have a good night. Maybe we'll run into each other again," Debbi said.

I got up from the bar stool, and headed for the door. I walked to my car and as I put my car key in the lock I thought about the girl I had just spent some time with in the bar. Then I headed off to my family.

Trina was awake when I walked in, and she wanted to know what I'd been up to. So I told her where I was, I didn't tell her everything that went on, I'm not stupid. She just nodded her head and said, "Uhm."

Should I have felt a little funny? I didn't do anything wrong.

Time was passing and the little man was crawling all over the place and attempting to walk while holding on to tables, chairs or anything else he could get his little hands on. By now my parents had bought some property with two houses on it, they lived in the front house and we lived in the back house.

One winter night I had gone to pick up Trina from work and just as we walked in my parent's kitchen door, little man was taking his first step. Man, Trina burst out crying and grabbed him up, liked to scared my poor child almost to death. My little sister Taz was holding a slice of apple out to him to get him to let go of the wall and walk. Well, it worked, from this point he was walking more and more.

Like most families we just did our normal little routine every day, then came home to observe the baby growing like crazy and getting into everything. He wasn't a bad baby at all, just always had something he had to do and get to.

It was Sunday morning, JoJo came over and we hung out around the house some this day. Man, we went got some liquor, beer and pickled pigfeet, then we came back had a drink or two, from here we went to my Uncle's for a minute to watch his son rebuild a race car. My cousin Dave had returned home and was now living four doors down from my uncle, he was helping our cousin rebuild this car. Let me tell you, these cats knew their stuff when it came to automobiles. If it had an engine they could handle it. As for me I can do the small maintenance stuff, but I don't like getting my hands dirty like that.

It was now Sunday afternoon, around four o'clock, we realized the time and we hauled ass back to my place to check out the games. I believe the Giants and the Cowboys were playing. Trina was heading out the door as we were coming up the porch steps,

"How are y'all doing, there's some food in there, help yourself. I'm going with your mother and Aunt Kate," Trina said to us.

We all said okay to her and I asked if she wanted me to keep little Allen while she was out, but she said no that was okay she was going to pick up a few things for him while they were out.

We were into the game when the door opened and my father came in to join us, not because he liked football, he just knew the guys were over and we were doing guy things. Pop and Uncle Ed had made some hoghead cheese, Pop ran to his house and came back with a huge piece on a plate with some crackers, as usual it was delicious. Our women had gone out to eat before they returned home, so they'd come back later than I expected them to, it was late enough for the baby to go straight to bed.

Monday came around and I went to work, already looking forward to Friday. You see my vacation started Friday evening, and so did Trina's, I was going to be off for a week and I planned to relax the whole week.

Friday came Dave and I had heard about a party around the way, so Dave and I stopped off at the spot, just to stick our heads in the door and check out what was happening. The party was hot, so I started having a good time, when who did I run into again, but Debbi. She and I danced a bit, drank a bit, talked and laughed a bit. You know, just jivin' and kickin' it.

Later that night, Dave and I decided to leave and head for home, Debbi had given me her phone number. I offered to drop her off on my way home, when I dropped Dave off. She accepted my offer so, I dropped Dave off first, then Debbi, she invited me in, so I went in for a while. One thing lead to another and before I realized it the sun was coming up so I got my ass out of there in a hurry. I kept thinking, Trina wasn't going to be happy about this shit and she might kick my ass today.

On the way home I was trying to think of an excuse, not just an excuse, but a good excuse. All I could think about was to say I was with the guys and got too drunk to make it home. I got home in about twenty minutes, there was a slight nip in the air, it almost helped me feel a little refreshed as I walked up the steps to the house. I inserted my key, the whole time I was thinking to myself, I hope she's not here right now, that'll give me some time to get myself together then I started opening the door. As soon as I stepped in Trina walked over from behind the door coming from the kitchen sink. "And where have you been," she asked?

"I'm sorry Trina, I was with the guys last night. We were hanging out and drinking, but I guess I had too much to drink and the next thing I knew, I was waking up and the sun was shining," I told her looking in her eyes hoping she would buy this shabby ass story.
"I half way don't believe you, but it's possible. Don't let this happen again, I mean it Allen," Trina told me as she roller her eyes at me.

I took the trash out, then came back in the house and sat on the sofa before I fell asleep for about two or three hours. When I woke up Lil'Allen was leaning on my side watching Saturday morning cartoons, Trina was on our porch with Mom, Aunt Kate and Taz. I finally got up and took Lil' Allen into the bathroom with me, so I could keep an eye on him while I was taking a shower. Lil' Allen loved water so I took him in the shower with me. Then we changed our clothes and joined the family outside. By the time we got out there, my Pop and Junie had came over too. Junie was saying he was going to pick up a sub (a submarine sandwich is a sub to us) then him and Paula were going down to the beach for a while.

It was close to lunchtime Pop went over to the big center block grill he had built, and started a fire so we could barbeque dinner. We cooked out almost every day as long as the weather was warm.

I do have to say it was a beautiful September day, not a cloud in the sky, a little humidity in the air, which made it feel warmer than it actually was. For some reason during this time of year, there were always hundreds of black birds in our neighborhood, squawking and filling the trees.

Junie got up to leave, of course we all kissed and hugged him, then we got in his bad ass Super Sport Chevelle and backed out the driveway. He had his car so clean it made me wash my new GTO, so the birds could shit all over it again by the next day.

I thought about who I had spent last night with. I knew I loved my wife and baby, Trina was beautiful, smart, sweet and could cook her ass off. I thought to myself I won't let that happen again. I still had seven more days off, maybe I would take Trina and the baby away for two or three days, that would still leave me a few more days to myself when we got back.

My Pop was going in the house to get some meat for the grill, Mom called to him to put on enough for Marie and Monica. They'll be over in a little while.

I called to Trina while I was washing my car, let's leave for Virginia tomorrow morning, to see your grandparents. We'll stay for two days, how's that?

"Really Allen, that sounds great. We can just throw a few things in a bag tonight. Let's leave around eight o'clock. You think that's a good time? We'd be there in about six hours," she said, all enthused.

"Sounds good to me babydoll," I replied back at her.

We didn't have to get anybody to keep an eye on that toe biting puppy, I had given him to some people I knew. So we were free to hit the road.

Marie............

Mike and I had gotten our divorce, he came to spend time with Monica regularly, and take her home with him to south Jersey every now and then, he was also allowed to have her for the Christmas holidays.

This one day he came to get her and we got into it. Fussing like mad, for some reason there was still tension and hostility there. Hell I hadn't done anything wrong to him or our relationship. I knew I was still hurt and mad at him. Finally we agreed to have him pick up Monica from my Aunt Kate's. I would drop her off with my Aunt then he'd pick her up from there. Mike loved my aunt, she was his angel, she could do no wrong in his eyes, to be honest, I felt the same way about her. He'd come to pick up Monica and visit Aunt Kate for hours, almost spend half the day with her, he'd even call her every now and then.

Autumn had come, the trees were beautiful shades of oranges, reds, yellows, golds and browns. Thanksgiving was next week, this was my favorite season of the year. The weather is cool, but that's okay, the trees make up for the coldness.

I was half way finished with beauty culture school and was doing hair for a few clients on the side. This one morning I was standing at my bedroom window looking out at a field across the street from me, sipping a cup of coffee and looking at the leaves blow, it was a little windy outside, but it was so warm and cozy in my place. Monica was in her playroom, I hadn't even turned the television on, I was just enjoying the peace and quiet of this morning and wondering what we would cook for Thanksgiving dinner.

Then the phone rang, I went to the phone in the kitchen, it was Momma. Her, Aunt Kate and I called each other every morning and every night, and half the time spent the time in between with each other. Anyway she said she was wondering what we would have for Thanksgiving.

"I was just looking out the window thinking the same thing," I laughed to her.

"You know we basically have the same thing every year. Turkey, gravy, stuffing, greens, candied yams, potato salad, turnips and sweet potato and apple pie," I said.

"I'm gonna have a ham this year too, we have more people this year. Trina will make the potato salad, Paula will bake the ham, I'll do the turkey, greens and stuffing, your daddy will make the candied yams and pies, and you do the turnips and greens." Momma said.

After the conversation, I got Monica and me ready for Momma to come and get us. Her, Aunt Kate, Taz, Monica, and I were going to the food store to shop for the week and for the holiday. Monica had her little coat, hat and gloves on, I had my coat by the door, so as soon as the horn blew, we'd dash down the stairs from our semi-project apartment. Aunt Kate and Taz were already with Momma and off we went to shop on this cold, breezy day.

I'm going be honest, after we had done all that running from store to store by the time we got back to my parents we were exhausted. We had picked up some cooked food for dinner, because our feet and legs were hurting before we even finished shopping. As we pulled up in the driveway Momma blew the horn for help unloading the car. Allen and Poppa came out to get the bags. I took Monica inside to let her take a short nap and to call this new guy I was seeing. I had met a new guy his name was Cory, the thing with this guy, he was fine, yet something wasn't just right, I mean he was really a sweetheart, but something lurked wrong in the background. I couldn't put my finger on it, to prove to myself if I was wrong or not. I figured until I was sure about this I should give him the benefit of the doubt, but take it slow. Cory and I made plans for tomorrow afternoon, so I told Momma I needed her to keep an eye on Monica tomorrow, I knew she'd say okay. We were here all the time anyway.

Anyway, Cory and I went out and by the time the date was over, I knew I had to end this. I still couldn't put two and two together, but I knew if I did the math, it wouldn't come out to equal four. I came out and told him that he was a very nice guy, but I wasn't ready for a relationship, I needed more time by myself to regroup, and he understood. Then he told me when I was ready to please call him.

Like I had said I love this time of year, so I had my place all decorated for autumn with the rich fall colors and my table was set like it was ready to serve a major Thanksgiving holiday feast on it. There were only two more days until Thanksgiving, so I started cooking some food for Monica and me to have here at our place the day after Thanksgiving. You know how you have to have leftovers from that meal. I was so glad we were out of school for the next couple of days, I needed the rest, and life had me tired. Nothing in particular was going on, just every day life had me tired. The day before Thanksgiving was a rainy, cold, breezy day, Momma had dropped Taz off to me. Taz and Monica were in the playroom all day, while I laid on the sofa sipped on some Vodka and orange juice while cooking all day, the apartment smelled so good and it was warm and cozy in here.
As you know Thanksgiving Day came and the family spent the day together, giving thanks, eating, watching football and sleeping.

Allen………..

Thanksgiving was fun as usual, it reminded me of when we were growing up and all living at home. I guess if we hadn't gotten married we wouldn't have moved out. My father wanted us to live at home until we got married, unlike lots of other parents that can't wait to have their kids move out.

Trina and I were doing okay, I haven't seen Debbi again, and Trina and my anniversary was just around the corner, a lot has happened in a year. My mother had told me not to get married just because Trina was pregnant, never try to correct one mistake with another mistake. I married Trina because I loved her and her being pregnant gave that extra little nudge I needed to ask her to marry me.

I was thinking all this while I looked at her asleep in the chair. Any minute now she would wake up and swear she wasn't asleep, that was her ritual.

It was about a week before our anniversary and Christmas. We were sitting in my mother's kitchen when we heard Taz telling Little Allen, no that's hot, don't touch that, then a pop sound, and another pop sound. We jumped up to run into the living room and get this baby. We ran to where they were and he was popping the Christmas lights on the tree with his bare little hand, he had no cuts or blood. By now it was so good to him he was pulling the Christmas tree down, and it was about to fall on him and he didn't even realize it. Trina grabbed him and I caught the tree before it hit the floor. We were amazed he could crush the light bulbs with his little hand, first the heat should have stopped him, second he shouldn't have been strong enough. Then my mother said that's the same thing you did when you were his age, popping the light bulbs.

On Christmas Eve, our anniversary we had made arrangements for the baby to stay with my Mother. Since we both loved Chinese food, we went to this nice Chinese restaurant that looked like it was in China. From here we went to the movies and home to be romantic. Can you believe before the night was over Trina went to get the baby, she said she didn't feel comfortable with him not being home. Anyway, the next day was Christmas day and my brother's birthday. We have quite a few Christmas babies in our family, me, I'm an Easter baby.

Christmas day the family gathered at my parent's house, we had visitors coming and going all day. Around our way, people celebrated the holidays for about two weeks, we started a half a week before Christmas and ended the celebration through the first weekend of January after the New Year. Family homemade wines were among our festive dishes, one of my favorites was hog headcheese and souse my father and Uncle Ed would have made. This New Year's Eve my Aunt Kate had a jumping party, man the music was pumping, we played pichino and cards, danced, drank, and laughed the night away. Aunt Kate's husband poured bottle after bottle of champagne to toast in the New Year. There were tons of my mother's side of the family in attendance. It was the middle of winter, and freezing outside, but inside the house was burning up from all the body heat, it was so hot we had the windows open and front door cracked. Did the neighbors complain about noise, you want to know? Hell no, they were partying with us.

After the holidays past everybody buckled back down and got back to work. It was the end of January when my boy JoJo reminded me of one of our boy's birthday bash coming up. I asked him if I should take Trina. He was like yeah, but the way he said it made me think twice about asking her. That night when I got in I did ask her if should wanted to go, gave her all the details of who might be there and how much fun it should be, but she decided to stay home, Trina was pretty much a homebody. I had decided I'd go, but wouldn't stay long, say about two hours. So the weekend of the birthday party came and I do say JoJo and I were looking kind of dapper when we entered into the party. When JoJo and I walked up the front steps of the porch, there were quite a few people on the porch, so we made our way inside. As soon as we made it in the door, we were handed drinks by some women in French maid outfits. We couldn't believe somebody had gone through all this, there was also a food spread out of this world in the kitchen, it looked like a restaurant buffet. I got a couple of dances with this hot looking chick that had a crush on me from high school. I told the girl I was dancing with I was going to get some food and something to drink, did she want anything. Well, she kind of shocked me by telling me she just wanted me. I smiled and played it off, then started making my way to the kitchen for some food. I was almost to the table, when a French maid handed me another drink, of course I didn't want to offend her so I gladly took the drink, then got me a plate of food. As I walked towards the side of the room to talk and eat, I felt someone looking at me, I didn't pay it much attention, just kept eating and talking. After I finished my food I went to get a beer and then headed back to the den where there were more people dancing, I got to talking to Dave and was laughing my ass off at something he had just said when someone asked me to dance. I looked to my side only to see Debbi. I asked her what was she doing here, she said her cousin had heard about the party so they stopped in for a few minutes. I took her by the shoulder and guided her to the dance area. We were still dancing, when Debbi's cousin came to tell her to come on it was time to leave. Before she left she asked me to call her, I told her I might. She was like, "Come on, call me when you get a chance." So

I finally told her I would, then she gave me a kiss on my lips and left.

Now, I do admit she crossed my mind again that night, I even kind of wished she was still here.

I did as I'd planned about not staying half the night here, I was home by one o'clock that morning. Which wasn't bad, I hadn't left home until nine thirty. The week past and I thought of calling Debbi, but knew I shouldn't, so I didn't.

Months past and one day Trina and the baby had gone to visit her mother for the weekend, I was setting around the house taking it easy, watching a good monster movie, when I decided it was time to give Debbi a call. Taz was watching television with me so I went upstairs to use the phone. Debbi answered the telephone and sounded surprised to hear from me.

"It took you long enough to call. I didn't think I'd hear from you," she said.

"I know. I've thought about calling, but you know how it is," I said to her.

We talked for a while, she wanted to know where I was calling her from. I told her home. She said, "I take it your wife's not home then."

"No she's away for the weekend," I told her.

"If you get too lonely let me know," she said.

I told her I'd keep that in mind, then ended our conversation. I did keep it in mind, but I didn't get too lonely, my little sister was pretty good company. She always came in the house every so often while she was outside playing, and we liked watching scary movies together, so I was pretty content with her companionship. It was going on ten o'clock when Mommy called out her back door for Taz to come in the house. She gave me a good night kiss and ran out the door to Mommy, I continued laying on the sofa watching television and snacking half the night until I went to bed.

Sunday afternoon, Trina called for me to pick her and Little Allen up from the train station, I stopped folding the laundry and went to pick them up. On the way back home Trina asked, "What were you doing when I called?"

I looked at Trina real serious and said, "I was folding laundry and you know how I hate to be disturbed when I'm folding clothes."

She looked at me like "yeah right" and fell out laughing.

Marie..............

Well, things were going fine for everybody. Paula was excited because her and Junie were going to start trying to have a baby soon, said she's getting all the practice she can get before they started working on the real thing.

For my excitement I was getting a new living room set and it's bad, gold and brown, a brown fuzzy sofa bed, with a gold wavy lounge chair and the tables are glass. Oh yeah, and big dark gold glass lamps, like the color of dark beer. My pad was going to be so nice.

I gave the old living room set to a neighbor, my brother Junie always said, "One man's trash is another man's treasure." Junie and Allen have also always told me not to worry about me and Mike, or any other man, because, when one bus leaves another one will be by in twenty minutes and the other saying went, if one won't another one will. So here I am waiting for another bus or the one that will, but in the mean while I wasn't holding my breath.

For now, I figured I would just date, but absolutely no going steady. I needed my time to study for school, and take care of Monica and myself. School was getting tougher, we were getting into chemicals and mixing chemicals. Each day after school I'd get Monica and go home and study, I really did enjoy cosmetology. As usual time was passing fast and I was getting closer to taking my state board test for cosmetology.

At this time my parents' owned three houses, they rented out two houses to my brothers with their families. Trina and Allen had moved into one house our parents owned, which was behind where my parents lived. Paula and Junie were living in the old house my folks had moved out of.

Anyway, one weekend Trina's father came to visit her, he considered himself to be a playboy. He was a little older and yes handsome, even seemed like a fun and nice guy. We all had a good time, of course we had cooked out and our neighbor next door and her boyfriend came over to cookout with us. My mother used to work with our neighbor, all of us were very close, they were our extended family. Anyway, that night Marvin had wanted to go out, he'd heard so much about this area, so he asked me to go with him. I didn't think anything of it, and was like yeah, that sounds good. He took me to my place to shower and change clothes, and then we were off. We went to a bar right down the highway from my folks, it was jumping, after this we went to another spot, where the Ohio Players were performing. We really had a nice time. I finally had him drop me off home around four that morning. Sunday afternoon I went over my parents house as usual, and he was there talking to them, he thanked me for such a nice time. I told him, maybe we could do it again if he comes down this way. He played it cool, never gave a hint that he was interested in me. Trina, Allen and the baby came over and hung out, Marvin was getting ready to head back to Massachusetts. Putting all his bad rags back in the trunk of his new white Cadillac, when he asked me for my number. I was like, "Fine here you go." Still not thinking he was interested in me, he's just a fun guy to hang out with. Then as I handed him my telephone number, he laid his smooth line on me and invited me up to Massachusetts anytime. "If you don't have a way up there, let me know and I'll make arrangements for you," he said, but he was sincere about making arrangements, I could tell. I just left it at that. I would have to talk to Trina about him and see what he was about first. A few days had past when Trina brought up the fact that her father asked about me. She asked me was I interested in him at all. I couldn't lie, he was attractive, and well groomed, and tailored clothes, you know you can tell when somebody really takes care of themselves. As she went on telling me about her father, I couldn't believe some of the things I was hearing about him. Things like he was not the best father, they weren't really close. He had a big beautiful home in Massachusetts, he takes good care of himself, and yes all the gold and diamonds on him are real, and then she told me the way he afforded all these things. Well, his house is really big, part of the house he uses to run as a whorehouse. As he would tell you it's not a whorehouse, it's an escort service. I was like stop it, really. She was like I'm serious about everything I just told you. After hearing his story from Trina, he came to visit a few more times, then can you believe I started dating him, not seriously, but he was an intelligent, worldly, handsome man that knew how to treat a lady and enjoyed doing so. Whenever he came down to visit we'd go out to the clubs, expensive restaurants, Atlantic City, go see stage shows, stay at very nice hotels, not that he was trying to impress me, he was accustomed to these types of things. We used to travel between Maryland and New York just visiting people and having a good time.

As time went on he kept asking me when was I coming to visit him. So after a while I gave in and agreed to check him out up there in a few weeks. That Friday night he came down to get me, then the next morning we got on Interstate 95 North headed for his place. We stopped along the way for lunch at some quaint little restaurant that overlooked the Hudson River. I swear this man knew some nice spots to go to. From there we continued on to his crib as he called it.

After we got into Boston on this tree lined street he started to slow his big Caddy up and turn into this driveway that lead to a gorgeous house, that had a flowered lawn that looked like it was professionally taken care of.

"Marvin, your home is really pretty," I told him.

"Well come on inside and make yourself comfortable. Let me know if there's anything you want, if it's not here, we'll get it," he said then came around to open my car door, he always did that. My brother Junie also always opened and closed a woman's door.

He opened his trunk to get my bags out and we went inside. Well, the inside was nicer than the outside. Thick plush carpet covered the floors, a huge fireplace greeted me as we walked into the den and there was also one in the living room. The furniture you had to see it for yourself, it was heavy quality furniture. The kind of furniture that if you got tired of it years from now, you could give it away and it would still be in top shape. There was a door he told me not to go in. I thought about what Trina had told me about what he did with part of the house, that must that part, I thought to myself. I just told him no problem. Even if you didn't want to be comfortable, this place just made you feel relaxed and so I did. There was a huge sloped lounge chair placed near the window, so I took the drink he had mixed for me and I went and laid back on the chair, gazing out the window every now and then, while we talked he had put on some Marvin Gaye in the background. After about an hour of laughing and talking he excused himself for about half an hour, said he had some business to take care of. He could probably see I needed a little nap from the look in my eyes. So while he was gone I took a nap, it was short, refreshing, and needed. I guess I was sleeping so good, he let me sleep for an extra half hour.

After I woke up, I admit I was kind of on the hungry side. When Marvin asked me if I was ready to eat, I wanted to grab him by his neck and scream, "Yes, for Christ's sake please let's eat. But instead I answered with, "Yes I am actually. What do you want for dinner?"
Let me tell you this man had done his thing, he had cooked dinner while I was sleeping. He'd steamed some lobsters, baked potatoes and made a great looking salad, had a strawberry short cake for desert. Do you think I could have gotten used to this? Yes I could have.

He had also invited a friend and his wife over for dinner. So I went to freshen myself up and changed clothes for dinner. The couple showed up and we had a few drinks before we went to the table to start dinner. After the delicious meal, we set around talking for about an hour before his friend suggested we go out for a while. I was gamed, going out sounded good to me. We grabbed our jackets and walked out to get in the car, his friend had a big, beautiful, black Mercedes setting out there waiting for us.

I'm not going to lie, I was a little impressed by all that was going on, but as we got in the car I wondered how this guy made a living. I was also trying to keep an eye on what went on around Marvin's house too. You know, like signs of men coming in and out of his house, suspicious looking things going on. So far I hadn't seen anything, but then again we were in a different part of the house.

The place we ended up at was a fancy underground type looking place. You know, it was a big house that had some of everything going on inside. Music, drinking, smoking and not just cigarettes either, pool tables, a gambling room, and some other rooms that we didn't check out, but the people here knew Marvin and his friend. The people treated us pretty good, I got the impression both Marvin and Scott ran a tab here, so some stuff was just put on Scott's tab and the other things were on the house for him and his guests.

The owner of the place made her way over to us and Marvin introduced me and told her where I was visiting from. There's going to be a fashion show here in two weeks,   the owner was telling us and then she wanted to know if I would be interested in modeling in the show. I told her I was from out of town and I was just here visiting. The owner had turned her attention to someone else for a minute. So Marvin looked at me and said, "You said that like you can't come back. You can make it to be in the show go ahead and tell her yes if you want to."

When she turned back towards us, I told her that sounds like it might be fun, but I have to check on something first and could I get back to her on that, by noon tomorrow. She was like, "Yes that'll be fine, Marvin has my number, give me a call in the morning. You'd make a good model, we'd be glad to have you participate."

By the end of the night I had checked out the place enough to decide if I'd do it or not, so the next morning I called to give her my decision, I told her I'd be able to make it. She gave me all the details, then asked if I would be able to make it to a fitting next Saturday, I told her I had to go back to New Jersey, but that I'd be here for the fitting. She said, "If things change and you can't come for the fitting, let me know right away so I can send the outfits to you by over night shipment and you have it fitted there for the show. I told her I'd keep her posted. Then for a minute I wondered why this woman I had just met, wanted me in the fashion show enough to send outfits to New Jersey. Sunday evening Marvin took me back to my place, he said he'd come and get me next Friday. I told him to let me get back to him on that, because I'd probably stay home and have those outfits tailored here, since I'd be away from Monica too much.

You know piece by piece, one step at a time things in my life were getting better. I was be finishing school soon, I'd gotten my social life together, my family life was great, and Monica's was doing great, thank God for all this. Actually, I'd already started doing hair on the side, that little money came in handy. Let me tell you I could do some hair, I could give the best perm on earth and put curlers in a head of hair that didn't have a perm and make that hair unkink and unfrizz.

One evening Allen and Poppa were in the den watching television, Momma was washing dishes, I was at the table with Paula and Taz, while Junie was going through the fridge when Paula said, "Mom, guess what me and Junie are doing."
Momma said, "What?"
"We're trying to make a baby," Paula said.
Junie turned red and started laughing, "Don't say that, why'd you tell," he said blushing.
He looked like a little boy blushing in front of his mother.
Momma dried her hands and hugged Junie. "That's fantastic," she was saying.
Allen came in the kitchen, "Did I hear that right," he asked?

Junie was blushing and still smiling, mean while Paula had this huge proud smile on her face.

Junie and Allen looked alike. Allen's poor little baby sometimes called both of them Daddy, because he couldn't tell them apart. A minute or two later Allen and Junie went in the den with Poppa to confirm what he'd overheard. About a half and hour later Aunt Kate came over to the house, she entered through the kitchen door with Monica. She had taken Monica with her to buy her a new coat. She bought quite a few of my baby's clothes, and as usual, they had stopped at McDonald's on the way home. Poppa didn't call Aunt Kate Wimpy for nothing, you know the little guy from Popeye that ate hamburgers all the time? Aunt Kate with her burger and fries and she was happy.

Junie............

Well, Paula and I were trying to start a family. I enjoyed making love to my wife, I knew she'd get pregnant some time soon. We had gone to the doctor, he had told us there's only a few days out of the month a child could be conceived. So to cut down on sex when she wasn't within those three days of conceiving, that way my sperm count would be up. Not that I had a low sperm count, but every little thing helps.

Man, she would make it a romantic happenin', candles lit all over the place, wine, good food even a seductive shower for two sometimes. The first two tries we didn't get pregnant, to be honest we both were kind of disappointed at this. The next month rolled around and we were going to give it another try. We went out to the Lobster Shanity, this is where she and I went once in a while for a special occasion. We had a great meal, wine even desert.

It had started getting a little dark, so we road down to the beach where I parked and all though the weather was cold we took a blanket out the trunk, then went down to set on a bench facing the ocean. She was soft and she looked soft, I couldn't keep myself from touching her. I caressed her rosy cheek, patted her ample butt which was soft yet solid at the same time, then down to her big thighs I rubbed. Her legs felt chilly so I covered us up with the blanket. The beach was barren this night, no one was on the boardwalk. After eating so much and my magic touch the ole' girl leaned her head on my shoulder with contentment. I nudged Paula so we could head back to the car, when she lifted her head off my shoulder she looked at me with those big greenish brown eyes, then she stroked my neck before kissing me. She started with my lips, then on to my cheek, my forehead, nose and back to my lips. You know, I was ready to leave the beach, so we could go for home and real romancing. We entered our apartment and headed for our big soft bed, where we undressed each other.

"Come on Big Daddy," she'd said.

You wondering why she called me Big Daddy? You know why. After a good session of passionate lovemaking we slept through most of the night, I woke up to go to the bathroom and get something to drink. While I was in the kitchen, Paula came in to get a piece of cake and some milk, then we took our snacks back to bed and watched the boob tube until we started another session of lovemaking up again. Needless to say, after the night we'd had, the next morning we both called our jobs to say we wouldn't be in today.

I had started going to college, so although I had taken a work day off I still went to school that night. Paula was to spend some time with Trina for a while.

Allen...........

It was a gorgeous day, so little Allen and I went visiting my Uncle J and Dave. My boy JoJo had gone to Texas and stayed after serving his time in the Air Force, from there he went to Seattle for a while. I missed that nut, we keep in touch, though. Anyway, Uncle J, my Mother's brother had ten kids, so his house was always busy. We went over to hang out with him first. Uncle J wore a suit seven days a week. No, not the same seven suits over and over again – he must have had over forty suits and hats to match along with shoes, of course. His hair was processed and curled, yeah, my man's hair was fried, dyed and laid to the side, and sometimes he had a red phone in his car, a stomp down house phone in his car. He was gold down not over gold, but enough to really be flashy, like the big medallion on his necklace. This day he was on the porch watching television with a house fan on the porch to make a breeze. We were having a drink or two, when his son and daughter Johnnie and Bebie came out and set with us for a few drinks, we just talked and watch people as they went by and enjoyed the breeze from the fan. After a couple hours I figured Little Man and I would on over to Dave's, I was putting my little man in the car, when Mom, Aunt Kate, Monica and Taz pulled up behind my car they were coming to check out Sammy Davis Jr. (aka Uncle J). Man, you know Sammy Davis Jr. had an eye that did it's own thing, well so did my Uncle J, so really with this and all the jewels, suits, hats, hair, Cadillac and car phones he earned this name, you see we called Uncle J, Sammie Davis Jr. Cool as hell and good hearted as they came, that was everybody's opinion of Uncle John.

Uncle John, Beebie, and Johnnie walked down to join us on the sidewalk, we all talked for two or three minutes, then the little man and me were off to Dave's.

Dave and Laurie had gotten married before Trina and I, they'd had a son after they got married, but they were having problems. The problem was Dave wasn't acting like a married man. As for me, I was trying my damnedest to act like a married man, but I swear some times it was so hard to do. Once in a while I wondered if we had gotten married too young. I loved Trina and I still do and we had this beautiful baby together, he's the best thing I've ever done. Then on the other hand, we hadn't sewn our wild oats, because he got married young. We went straight from high school to the war, to marriage and a family. We went from being schoolboys, to being war soldiers and then directly to being husbands with mouths to feed. I'm glad for my family, just sometimes wish God had given this to me after I'd had a chance to enjoy being a manboy. A manboy, that's a mix of still some boy inside and being a young man; it's time to explore myself and the world around me.

I held little Man's hand as we walked to Dave's door, Laurie answered the door, she said Dave wasn't home, hadn't seen or heard from him since early this morning. So she and I sat on the porch for a short while talking and watching the people in the neighborhood. She offered us some iced tea and I was glad to get some, I guess that liquor had made me thirsty. While she went to fix the glasses I changed Little Allen's (Little Man) diaper. Gloria my cousin from a few doors down was walking by and came over to join us. Laurie came out with our iced tea, then had to go back to get a glass for Gloria. This time she was smart she brought the whole pitcher with her when she came back. The three of us drank tea and talked and gossiped, while our little boys played on the porch.

Since Dave wasn't home that had blown my plans of having a few drinks with him, dropping my son off at home, then having a couple of guys over to hang out for us to go out. So on my way home I made a stop at a phone booth to give Debbi a call, her roommate answered the telephone, she called Debbi to the phone for me. We made plans to see each other later that week. I figured that would give me enough time to back out of it or either get the nerves to go through with it.

That Monday when Trina and I had gotten in from work she told me we were invited to a cookout, a girl she worked with invited us. Well, that Saturday we went to the cookout. I admit it was nice, tons of food, liquor, music and fun, we even played dodge ball. Can you picture some grown ups running, ducking, dodging and throwing a bouncy ball around after having a few too many drinks and having full bellies of food. It was hilarious, man, and the next day we were sore and stiff as hell.
Trina and I took turns massaging each other trying to get rid of some of the soreness.
Us massaging each other, turned into two sore stiff people making love, but for reason while we were making love I didn't feel the sore and stiffness. I played basketball pretty often, but some how the action at the cookout was different to my body, because after Trina and I finished we were back to being stiff and sore.

Man, each day was passing, it was getting closer to the day me and Debbi are supposed to go out. I was getting nervous, but I went through with it and we got together for drinks. I picked her up at her place and we rode out to a nice quiet spot in Brielle on the river, where nobody knew me. Again we enjoyed each other's company, we went for a ride, then I decided I'd better drop her off at home. As we pulled up to her door in the apartment complex, she asked me in. I didn't want to hurt her feelings, so I said alright. When we got inside she realized her roommate wasn't home, we sat on the sofa, while watching television I started rubbing her knee and lower thigh and a quick snack turned into me leaving there about three hours later, telling her I'd call her.

Marie...........

Remember I didn't go to Massachusetts for the fitting, but I made it there for the fashion show. They had sent me three outfits to model and I thought of different hairstyles to go with each outfit. I had never been in a fashion show before, it was fun and a lot of excitement was going on back stage. Women putting on make-up and hair, changing clothes, laughing and the designers were in an uproar fixing their creations to perfection on their models. The men were in a room right next door, we'd see some of them running back and forth in a frenzy getting ready also. The music was playing and it also helped keep us hyped off stage and on stage. Nobody could tell us we weren't big time modeling professionals. It was my turn to strut out, I was nervous and praying I wouldn't trip, fall or anything like that. Once I walked out and made the turn into the lights, I was still nervous, but I also thought to myself, go on girl you gotta do yo thang now, so I strutted down the runway, throwing my hips from side to side, with my head looking straight forward. The show went on for about an hour. Then following the show we were backstage removing the exaggerated make-up and hair, while people were coming backstage to talk to us about doing shows for them and speak with designers about their clothes. I was asked to do a show. Let me tell you, I had so much fun doing this one, I agreed to model for a show in Baltimore, also the pay wasn't bad doing these shows either.

Out front, where the audience was, people were standing around drinking and talking and setting up deals.

We hung around for a little while, Marvin was cool, but I could tell he was proud of me. While Marvin and I were setting at the bar sipping on drinks and talking about all that was going on in the place, a guy of average height and very handsome, I couldn't tell if he was Greek or Italian came over and asked me who was my hair stylist. I told him I had done my styles myself. He said he was from Italy and had been in the United States for the last couple of months promoting hair shows mostly on the east coast and was wondering if I might be interested in participating in one of his presentations. I was like, "Of course, why not. Just get back to me when you have everything pretty much lined up, so we can discuss the details." I gave him my number and he gave me his business card. I was finding this whole fashion show thing to be exciting, and now a chance to do a hair show, I could dig this for a while.

The next morning I hurried back home having missed class today, I still had so much to do this week, including school and the show in my hometown this coming weekend.

Mike had left Monica with my Aunt Kate. After arriving at the train station I called for a taxi to go pick up my baby and get started with my week.

Junie................

Marie had come home and told us about her fashion show and how it turned out, now she was going to participate in a hair show. I decided I had to check out what she was doing and who she was dealing with, so I told Allen about the hair show and that maybe we should check it out. He was like, "Man, a hair show. That's for women."

"No it's not just for females she says it will have male hair modelers too, after the show there'll be drinks and dancing afterwards," I told him.

The look on his face said he wasn't really excited about it, neither was I, but at least it was something different to do, and we'd be checking Marie out. He agreed it would be nice for us to go, so we could give her our support and it might be a little bit of fun in it. We then agreed to tell our wives about this, even though we didn't know the date or place, we just knew we'd be there. Paula and Trina were excited about going. Paula started planning what she was going to wear to the show already. I told her to relax, we don't even know when the show is going to be. A few days later Marie called Paula and Trina about the hair show, she wanted to know if they'd like to be her models. She needed three models, she already had Leya as a model. Of course, Paula was gung ho about being in the show and told her yes, almost before Marie could even finish asking her. The more talk I heard about this event the more fun it sounded like it might be. It was going to be a group of us going, even my cousin and wife from Baltimore said they'd come to the show, whenever it was going to be. I'd say it was about two and a half weeks after Marie had told us about this, when she got a call from the guy that was running the show. After Marie spoke with him she called her models to give them the details. Now listen to this, the show was going to be in Baltimore, so now we made plans for convoy of cars to go down there, even my Mom and Dad were going. As I pretty much went about my daily routine, the women were practicing walking, discussing what they were going to wear, how the make-up should be applied, you know all that kind of stuff. Us men didn't have to go through all that hassle. That's not the truth either you know, Allen, Dad and I had talked about what we were wearing too.

Time was passing pretty fast as I watched them prepare for the show. You know how it is when you can feel the excitement of an event. The next thing we knew it was almost time to leave for Baltimore, it was two days before the show down. Man, we had a convoy of cars going down, let's see there was four to a car, and we had three carloads heading down 95 South. It wasn't really a long ride, it only took three and half to four hours to get there, but we stopped half way there to freshen up, stretch our legs and talk of course. Normally my folks stayed at my cousin's house, so my mother and father stayed with Rob and Shelley, but there were too many of us for us all to stay with them this weekend. So the rest of us had made reservations at the hotel where the show was taking place, the spot was really nice, it even had an indoor pool. The hotel had given us a discounted rate, because my sister was a stylist for the hair show.

Four hours after leaving New Jersey we arrived in Baltimore and went straight to Rob and Shelley's place. We hadn't seen them in a few months, so there was a lot of talking going on, catching them up on what was happening in Jersey and them updating us on what had been happening in Maryland. They had a nice place, ranch style home with a finished basement, and a huge yard and their bar in the finished basement was fully stocked as usual. After our ride, we stayed for a short while before going to the hotel, the women needed to prepare for tonight. Mom and Dad stayed with our cousins. We arrived at the hotel, there were quite a few people in the hotel for this show and afterparty.

Marie, Trina, Paula and Leya women were doing make up and hair for a few hours, before they went down to go back stage to start getting dressed for the stage, I'd say they went down around five thirty, although the show didn't start until seven. The seats in the room were filled when the curtain opened, the first thing to happen all these beautiful women came out strutting around the stage were these wild, and I do mean wild lavish colorful outfits, with huge hats, plumes. After this some models with strange yet sexy make-up came back out again, this time wearing hardly anything, I mean, tight fitting dresses and pants, halters, hip hugging pants, their stomachs, backs and half their breasts out. I admit I was like wow, I could get used to seeing this, but they didn't look tacky, they looked sexy and glamorous.

The show was really good, it was amazing the things that could be done with hair.

Allen and I were kind of hoping Paula and Trina might leave their hair looking wild and exotic with that far fetched make-up for later tonight when we returned to our hotel rooms. The place was going to be jumping almost until the sun came up, but we'd had a ball, then most of our group turned in somewhere around four that morning.

The next afternoon after we had tried to sleep off our tiredness and the liquor we'd consumed the night before, we made our way to Cousin Rob and Shelly's. It never failed, whenever we came down they'd get a ton of already cooked crabs. So while Shelley called to place the order for the crabs, so her and Mommy could go pick them up, Allen, Dave and I started ripping open some paper bags and placing them on the dining room and kitchen tables. Meanwhile Rob walked over to his stereo and turned on some Al Green while he was talking to Dad. After this Rob went down to the bar to bring up a few things, most of us had gone out into his huge backyard, to see if things were still the same. The house sat up on a slight hill, so you looked down into the yard and over to the street behind him. His yard was lined with tall hedges, a giant brick grill, and patio furniture.

Let me tell you though, as soon as Shelley's car pulled up in the driveway we went into the kitchen all of us moving around getting butter, napkins, glasses, and anything else we thought we might need to damage to these crabs. Ice cold beer, crabs and good conversation, yep, that was a usual here. While we were eating, Shelley's brother Henry came in with his wife and a friend of his, they had also attended the bash last night.

Allen.........

Well, well, well, I wasn't expecting to enjoy a hair show, I was going just to keep an eye on my big sister and give her support, but I can truly say, I enjoyed the show and the after party. Man, everything was solid. Seeing Trina looking fixed up in that hair and crazy make-up with that skimpy dress had made me feeling real good.

I guess the excitement of the show and us getting away for an exciting weekend helped Trina and I to have some much needed fun, so when we got back home I thought I wouldn't call Debbi again. I was hoping this feeling that was in our home would stay just this way. You know that little tingly warm feeling, and that warm tingly feeling did stay for a while, or at least three or four weeks. Trina and I were in bed watching television while the baby was in his crib almost snoring, and I was thinking to myself, we'd been arguing off and on, maybe we're just in a rut. We'd been doing the same thing day in and day out, it was making us lose the thrill of being together. Trina had gotten up to get a magazine to read while watching television, I drifted off to sleep thinking maybe we're just in a rut. Tuesday morning we woke up to do our usual routine of getting ready for work and getting the baby ready, me kissing them both before I walked out the door to get in the car to go to work. Trina didn't drive and had no desire to learn, that I didn't understand, because she liked to go places. Anyway, after I left for work, about an hour later she'd go over to Mommy's. Mommy would drop off Little Allen at the baby sitters first, drop Taz off at school which is just around the corner from the babysitter, from there she'd drop Trina off downtown at the phone company, then she'd swing herself to work which was also a few blocks from the babysitter's. I got home before Trina so some times I'd to pick something up for us, pick up the baby and then it off to pick up Trina. You know the daily drill was going on again. As time passed, unfortunately, things had gotten back to it's normal. I started going out a bit more, and a little bit more and a little bit more. And yes, I had seen Debbi two or three times. Now get this, somehow she had found out where I lived, that shit wasn't cool. She mentioned to me that she knew where I lived, I said in a playing way, but really to myself it was a hopeful way, "You do not."

She said, "Yes I do, I saw you one day as I was leaving Dunkin Donuts, we were pulling out the exit as you went by us at the light, so I told the girl I was with to follow your car.

Well, the girl wasn't lying, she did know where I lived and what my family looked like. I thought to myself, I hope I hadn't started any shit here. At the same time I didn't let her think it bothered me that she knew this bit of info on me. Sometimes if you let someone know something they know or did bothered or worried you, they hold it over you. We saw each other again about two weeks after the occasion where she told me she knew where I lived. Let's see, it was a Thursday night when we got together this time and everything was good. The next day, which was Friday I went to work as usual, came home and hung around there for a while. A friend of mine called to ask me to come over and watch a game with him, so I was like sure. I went around to my parent's front porch where the family was setting, watching people and cars go by so I could tell Trina I was going over to Steve's to watch the game. I had already had a sip or two of wine before I left the house, and on my way to Steve's house I stopped around the corner and some liquor to take with me so we could make drinks for the game.

When I got to his house there a few other guys there, we drank, watched basketball, and yelled at the players the rest day into the night. Once while I was watching the game I thought about the argument Trina and I had earlier in the day.

Marie...........

I had somehow gotten myself so busy, being a divorced mother, going to school, working part time, doing shows, and doing every day things.

Mike would come get Monica some weekends, he'd call my Aunt Kate and schedule information. If it was good with Monica's and my schedule she could go, if not he'd make other arrangements to take her another time. In our divorce we agreed to let him have her for the Christmas holidays and two or four weeks out of the summer. I admit he was good about taking his daughter and spending time with her, yeah he was a good father, even if he was a poor ass excuse of a husband. When he could pick her up, then Aunt Kate would give me the message.

Time was just whipping by, I had been so busy. I received a call from the woman from Boston about their show coming to Asbury Park soon. She was telling me after hearing where I was from after talking to her partners they were interested in me participating in the show at the

Convention Hall in Asbury Park. I thought, heck that's the next town over from where I lived. A lot of big shows in the entertainment business went on there. Now I've heard it's about to be right in my own backyard, this could be outrageous fun about to happen. Over the next week I had pretty much told everybody I knew about the show and where and when it was going to be. I had three months to prepare for this show. To be honest I needed at least three months to line things up and try to finish school.

I could have between three to six hairstyles displayed in the show. I chose to have four, that way I'd be able show short and long hairstyles, braids, and naturals, but having six styles seemed to be pushing a little too much, because during the second half I'd be modeling two outfits. Now I had to round up my models again, I had to see if they wanted to be down. The people I thought to use for the show wasn't because they were my favorites, they had the hair pretty much the way I could use it or they wouldn't mind me cutting and coloring their hair if necessary, I enjoy showing my versatility.

Mike hadn't taken Monica for a weekend in the last couple of months, but he was coming to get her this Friday. I had her little suitcase packed, so she was ready to go. Him picking her up for a weekend every now and then gave me some time to myself, but a weekend was enough time, because by Sunday afternoon I was missing my baby kind of bad.
Marvin was talking about coming down to see me for the weekend, but I asked him not to. I explained to him how busy I had been lately and how I needed some time to myself to completely unwind and relax. He was disappointed and almost a bit agitated, but he tried to hide it. Another minute or two of talking and he had gotten over being agitated, but he was still disappointed, but he

also told me he completely understood me needing time to myself. He's so darn understanding, I thought to myself. If he lived close by I'd be glad for him to come over for two or three hours, but not for the whole weekend. So it had to be nothing or all weekend, I stuck with the nothing at all. My telephone had a really long cord, so while he and I were running our mouths on the phone, I started getting Monica ready for bed. She was able to do it herself, I thought to myself, God she was growing up. She did mostly everything herself, I just checked and double checked her to make sure it was done right. Except for her wiping herself after going to the potty, that was still my job, the clean up. Let's see it was about thirty minutes later when Marvin and I hung up the phone for the night. I tucked my little girl in bed, then got myself ready for bed also. Tomorrow Monica would be leaving for the weekend, and I was excited about taking a long hot bubble bath Friday night and laying in bed studying for my finals and sleeping off and on through the night. You know how it is, no schedule, so you take catnaps when you want to.

Friday afternoon Mike came to Aunt Kate's and picked up Monica. As they got ready to leave the apartment, I kissed Monica and told her to be a good girl and Mommy will see her in a few days. She didn't cry when we went through this routine, she was happy to go spend time with her father, but on the other hand when she was ready to come back home, she'd pick up the phone in a minute to let me know it. I then told Aunt Kate thank you for everything and asked for a ride to Momma's. Aunt Kate dropped me off in front of the door, I walked up the driveway past my mother's and father's house to my brother Allen's to see how they were doing. Trina and Little Allen were home, "Oh, you're on your way out. I was just stopping in to see how you're doing,"

I said as I picked up the baby so I could get some kisses from him. He was a sweet little smiley thing. Trina said, "I was just going with Gloria for a while. Shopping and stuff like that." "Alright then, I won't be here when you get back I'm just dropping by for a little while. You still going to do the show, right," I asked?

"Heck yeah, I still want to do the show. It's going to be fun, because so many people we know will be there to see it," Trina was saying as Little Allen played with my lips. I told her, "I'll keep you posted. In a few days I'll want to try a hairstyle out on you. Let me know when will be a good time for you."

We started out the door to the porch, Gloria had pulled up in the driveway and tooted the car horn. My parent's back door flew open and Taz stuck her head out to speak to Gloria and Trina for a minute. I talked to Gloria for a minute, she reminded me to tell her more about the show, and after this I went in the door that Taz was holding open for me.

Momma, Poppa, Taz and I sat around the kitchen table for some time eating and talking while half way listening to the television in the other room. Finally, about five thirty I asked Momma to give me a ride home, and as usual she did. She, Taz and I got in her Chevy, I turned on the car radio and we slowly rode down the ave to see the sights and people, then we rode past the beach and boardwalk to see what was going on down there too. Then we made our way to my place, where I said good night to them. I went inside my little sanctuary of peace and quiet, where I was about to have some time all to myself. I enjoyed the quietness for a while once inside, a little later I turned on my television in the bedroom, strolled in the kitchen to the counter at the sink, then I reached up in the cabinet to get a glass. Then the telephone rang and I reached across to the wall opposite the sink for the phone, it was Marvin. We talked as I opened the refrigerator for ice, vodka and orange juice and started to mix a screwdriver.

After making my drink I went into the living room and laid up on the sofa while we ran our mouths for a while longer. I thought to myself, heck I could run my tub water and load it with bubble bath while I'm on the phone. I'd had a not so pleasant experience as a little girl with some tub water, so now I only ran about three inches of water in the tub. I would drain the tub and run more water in it several times while bathing.

"Is that water I hear," Marvin asked me?

I told him yes, I was going to take a hot bath and get in bed, watch television and let the breeze blow across me. I always had a nice cross breeze, I guess because I didn't live far from the beach.

"See if I were there you'd have somebody to wash your back. There better not be anybody else washing your back," he said chuckling.

One thing I had to give him, he was self-assured of most things, not insecure this made me feel comfortable with him, because he wasn't intimidated by me being myself in any way.

At this point in our relationship, I had figured out that Marvin ran a whorehouse, or as he'd say upscale escort service.

I finished talking with Marvin, let the water out of the tub then ran more fresh water to soak in for a minute without the bubbles in the water. The water was feeling so relaxing I was tempted to run a third bath to soak in, but I didn't I was actually ready for the comfort of my big soft mattress. So I got out the tub and dried myself off, applied some lotion, grabbed my sexy nightgown, that's all I owned, then proceeded to the kitchen to freshen up my screwdriver. From here I headed straight for my bed, where my books and the television were waiting for me.

Junie...........

    I had finally gotten Paula pregnant before we had gone to Baltimore, but now Paula was showing pretty good and I was always rubbing her stomach. Yeah, yeah, she's a bit spoiled, but she spoiled me back. She was giving sweets hell and was saying how she wanted to be in this show that was coming up, but at the same time wasn't really up to it and had gotten too big. I was still working, going to school, and trying to keep the ole girl comfortable. I said to her, "Here's some money, find yourself some fancy maternity clothes."
"Thank you," she said, "I know where to find something."
She wasn't telling me anything new, I knew she had seen something she wanted.
    I had just come in from school one night, Paula was on the sofa running her mouth on the phone eating a can of chocolate cake frosting, by the spoonfuls. Just looking at her eat that sweet stuff was turning my stomach. She came over and gave me a kiss, then I went to the bedroom. She got off the telephone and came to see what was going on with me and how was my day. I got up off the bed and went into the bathroom to run some water over my hands and face and she was right behind me, just talking. We ate dinner, she had cooked spaghetti, salad, and garlic bread, the meal was dynamite.
I told Paula I was tired, I had been tired more often since she had been pregnant. My mother told me this was normal, lots of times when a woman was carrying, the father of the baby would experience some symptoms. I ate and sat down for about twenty minutes then told her

to, "Come on, let's go ride by the ocean before I come back and go to sleep."

The next day Paula and I went in to the doctor's office for her check up, and everything was great with her and the baby. Man, I'm tickled about having a baby.

I pray no matter what it is boy or girl, that it just be healthy, but if it were a boy I'd be so happy I don't think I'd know what to do with myself.

Allen................

We'd been living behind my parents for about a year now, in a house they owned.

I was still over Steve's, the game was still on, another hour and I'd head home. I'd say it was close to eleven o'clock when I got home, when I walked in, Trina was furious, I mean like nothing I'd ever seen before. I walked in the door, I asked her what was wrong. She just looked at me, "Your bitch was here, she came to the house."

I said, "Trina what are you talking about"?

"That white tramp you've been seeing came here tonight. Walked right up to my door, knocked and walked right in, asking to see you. I first thought about kicking her ass for being so brazen, but decided you're the one that needs to be fixed. So I let the bitch live to walk out of my house."

"Who came here," I asked confused and scared.

"You know who came here. Don't pretend you don't know what I'm talking about", Trina said.

I decided to say, "I saw her only a few times, there's nothing going on, Trina. I know what I did was wrong, but please forgive me. She must have come here, because she was mad that I hadn't been seeing her."

"You know you're wrong, there's nothing to even fuss about. Just leave me alone", she told me.

I walked out into the yard, where Taz was setting on the back porch. At first I didn't even see her there, and she didn't say anything, I just realized there was somebody out there with me. So I looked around and spotted her, I asked Taz, did anybody come to my house while I was gone. She told me, "Yes, I was here on the porch, when a white lady came walking up the driveway and asked me were you home. I told her no. Then she went to your house knocked on the door and before Trina could answer she opened the door and walked in. I couldn't hear what they were saying in the house, but the white lady didn't stay long, a few minutes later she came out and walked down the driveway then made a left heading for the highway."

From here I went to set on the front porch with my mother to give Trina more time to herself. Mom told me some white girl had gone back there, but it seemed like Mommy had no idea what had gone on. I spent another hour on the porch before I went back in the house with Trina and the baby. He was sound asleep and Trina had gotten in the bed too.

I took a bath, then got in the bed beside Trina, I was being very careful not to wake her. I wanted to touch her, but I knew not to. She had been so upset she didn't even really fuss or have too much to say about what had happened. I laid there thinking for some time, how I had to call Debbi to tell her about coming here, I wanted to kick her ass, but I was in the wrong, right along with her.

Morning finally came, it had been a long night for me. We woke up and I asked Trina to please forgive me, I'd make it up to her. She answered me with, "I'm leaving you. You take some time to figure out what and who you want. I'll give you seven years to get it together."

Her decision had come just from Debbi showing up here, before Debbi showed up she and I had been arguing and fighting several times.

Still, I was almost in shock when she said this. I had to go to work, maybe I should have taken this day off, but somehow I wanted to get away to try to see what the hell I was thinking and give me a minute to think. I told Trina I wanted to talk things over when I got in from work. I kissed her and gave a long hug, before I went into Little Allen's room to get a kiss from his soft little cheek. Then off I left for work, thinking the whole way to work about last night, this morning and what to say and do this evening when I got home. First thing I did after I got in the door to my job, I headed for the telephone to call this bold chick that just walked in on my wife and baby. Debbi answered the telephone, I asked, "What in the hell made you go to my house last night?"

"I felt like letting her know about me. It was time for you to decide what you wanted," she said.

"Why didn't you speak to me about this," I asked.

"I've asked you a couple of times, you'd always try to find a way to buy more time. I got tired of waiting", she said to me.

"Look we shouldn't see each other anymore. My shit is fucked up at home now, and I have to straighten it up", I told her. Then I hung the phone up before she could even say anything else.

This day at work was going even slower then usual. Then just my luck they wanted me to work a double. I found somebody to work it for me, I had to get my ass home.

I was holding my breath on the way home, thinking I hope Trina's still there, and how were things going to turn out with our talk. Thank God when I got home she and the baby were still there. We talked things over and she agreed to hang in there a while longer and try to give me another chance. I'd say it was a week later, when I went out drinking with the boys, and had the audacity to come home running my mouth too much and to loud. I'd never been one to hit on women, but I grabbed Trina. Why I don't know, the only way I could explain it was I'd been drinking.

Things weren't good for us at home, there was tension there. Tension of her not liking what had been going on, being hurt, and being disappointed. Tension of me having done wrong, hurting and disappointing her and the question of, is this going to work and what can I do to make it work. It had been two weeks since the incident of Debbi showing up at the house, when Trina told me she wasn't happy living like this. Again she told me she was going to leave and she'd give me some time to figure out what I wanted to do. Seven years she gave me to decide, seven years she'd wait. I told her I didn't want her to leave, I wanted her and our baby.

That Tuesday I went to work and I had a game that evening at six, so I went straight from work to the courts. I had told Junie about my situation, he tried to give me some advise. Anyway, I finally got home about nine-thirty that night from the game and my house was empty. I mean not just Trina and little Allen were not there, but the baby's furniture and their clothes were gone. I couldn't believe this. I ran out the house over to my parents to see if they knew what was going on. My mother told me to sit down she'd tell me everything that happened. Trina had talked to her mother and made arrangements to go live with her. She had a few people come with a truck come and she packed their clothes and the baby's things, she didn't want to take anything you might need, we helped her pack the baby's furniture and they left. She said you know where she would be staying and that she'll call you.

I was furious and I was crying. Mommy calmed me down and said, I was doing the things a married man shouldn't do.

"Trina was right to leave and give you time to get it out of your system, I know I should have left your father years ago," Mom said. Then she made me a plate of food and sat it on the table in front of me. "Go on and eat something. She'll call you, if she don't get an answer at your house she'll call here."

I had started eating my food quietly thinking to myself. When I heard the telephone ringing at my house I jumped up from the table, ran out the back door, jumped down the porch stairs, and ran across the yard to my place to get to the telephone. It was Trina, she kept her word, she called me just like she said she would. No matter what I said or how I asked, she stuck with not coming back right now. We talked about me seeing little Allen as often as I wanted. Even with me hurting her, she was still considerate of my needs when she packed so she left me everything, left all the furniture except the baby's things. She was going to live with her mother, so she didn't need any of the furniture, but she could have been nasty and taken the furniture anyway and put it in storage or sold it. Something on that order, you know? Well, we talked for a few minutes and when we ended this conversation, she still wasn't coming right back, told me to get this out of my system then we'd take it from there. Days past and I did my regular thing of working, hanging out and thinking about Little Allen and Trina. Days turned into two weeks, I called Trina and told her I wanted to come see Little Allen, she was like that's fine, when will you be here. I told her I had changed jobs and was now doing security work, so I'd be there tomorrow around three or four that afternoon. I had to go to work tomorrow at midnight.

I got in from work at seven thirty in the morning., got me a little shut eye until one thirty in the afternoon. I got up and turned on the radio to WBLS, they were playing my jam by the Dramatics, so I turned it up a little that way I could hear it all over the house while I got my self together. I opened the door, it was a bit cool, but that was alright, I had the storm windows in the outer door, this would let the sunlight in but not let that cool air inside. I walked into the bathroom and started running the water for my bath, when the telephone rang, I didn't bother to answer it. I guess it was about two minutes later, somebody knocked at my door, I put my robe back on and went to answer it. It was my mother, I was always happy to see her, so I was smiling while I opened the door to let her in, "Hi, come on in I was just about to step into the tub when you knocked," I told her.
"I called but didn't get an answer, I knew you were up, because I saw your door open," Mommy said to me.
"I'm getting ready to go to see Trina and Allen, from there I'll go to work. I got my uniform and everything I'll need to leave from her place," I was telling Mom, as I was already back in the bathroom getting into my nice hot tub of water. The bathroom was right off from the kitchen, so I left the door cracked so we could talk. My mother, oh you can talk to her about any and everything, both her and my Pop were easy to talk to. I was getting out of the tub, drying myself off so I could put my robe back on. I was almost finished, I just had to dry off my back then put my robe on Mom started saying she was about to leave. I told her to hang on a minute I was on my way out there. I finished putting on my robe and walked out into the kitchen, she was standing over at the kitchen door looking out.
"Want me to make you something to eat real quick before you get on the road," she asked?

"No, that's okay I'll grab some McDonald's before I get on the parkway," I told her.

Mommy said, "Well, be careful on the road and give them my love and tell her to come down here to see me. I'm gonna go back home now, so you go ahead and get ready and I'll see you tomorrow morning. If you want to come over in the morning, I'll have breakfast ready."

"See you about seven thirty then", I said and gave her a kiss on her forehead before she started out the door.

I continued getting ready to leave. I was on my way to my car when Taz came riding up in the driveway on her bike. "Can I ride with you," she wanted to know? I told her where I was going and she wanted me to tell them she missed them. I told Taz, "I'll tell them for you."

She stuck her head in the open window of the car to give me a kiss on the cheek. The radio was on and already tuned to WBLS in my GTO as I backed out the driveway. Since McDonald's was just around the corner from my house I pulled up to the drive thru window to place my order, "I'll take a large order of fries, a big Mac, a large coke and an apple pie", I told the girl at the window. I got my order and I headed for the parkway north.

The ride was pleasant, it was mostly sunny a few drifting clouds, and it had gotten a little warmer since this morning. As for me, a drive can sometimes help me to think, it gives me time to think, if traffic is light. Today traffic was very light, I think probably, because it was the middle of a weekday. Before I knew it I had gotten to my exit, so I pulled over to the right lane so I could exit and throw my dime in the exact change basket of the tollbooth. With as many cars that go up and down this road you know it's been paid for, what does the state do with all the money they're making from the tolls, I wondered as I threw my dime in. Actually, I was a bit nervous and a bit anxious to see them. You know me, the last light before I arrived in front of their door, I glanced in the mirror to see if I looked fine and check to see if my mouth and teeth had any remaining food on them. I was cool or able to play it cool, by the time I wove my way through the traffic of the city to get to the apartment they were staying in. I pulled up in front of their door and sat there for a few seconds, then took a deep breath before I opened my car door to step out. By the time I walked around the front of the car, Trina opened the apartment building door as I stepped onto the curb. She looked like she was happy to see me, but didn't want to show it and like she wasn't quite sure how to act.

To be honest, I was feeling the same way. I wanted to hug her and give her a kiss, but felt that would have been inappropriate. So after we entered the apartment building, I just bent over after we entered the hallway of the apartment building and gave her a kiss on the cheek. "Come on up, he's watching Sesame Street. That's his favorite, can't get him from in front of the television, while that's on", she was saying as we walked toward the steps that would take us to the second floor of the building. It's not polite, but as she lead the way up the steps I had to look at her behind, lovely it was and lovely it still is. When we entered the door of the apartment, he wasn't there, but we had to walk into the next room, there he was planted on the floor paying close attention to what they were doing on Sesame Street. I said, "Hey there little man", he jumped up and into my arms. He looked just like me, except he had green eyes like his mother. We hung out there in the apartment for a while, then I took them out for dinner, nothing fancy. Chinese food, yes it was of course. Then back to the apartment, I told Trina I was going to leave at seven thirty, that way I could get to work early so I could take a nap before my shift started.

By this time her mother had come home, she and I were never fond of each other. She didn't like me before she even met me. Come to find out she had a little distaste for most people. Trina insisted I take my nap here in the bedroom that she and the baby slept in. Said she'd be watching television for a while anyway, she pointed to the bedroom door and I wished she would come in there and lay with me, but hey at least I was spending time with the both of them. "You sure this won't be a problem", I asked her.

"No, it won't be a problem, now go on", Coffee and Cream told me.

"I'd better go to the car and get the things I'll need when it's time for me to get ready for work", I said.

So I headed for the car, I felt a bit uplifted as I walked out the door.

I got my things, then came back inside, Trina was getting Allen ready for bed. She was just coming out the bathroom carrying him, then I went in to sponge off some before I laid down. She had put Allen in his crib when I came into the bedroom, "He won't bother you. You know he'll be sleep in two or three minutes", she said.

"He'll be fine. Would it be a bother if you could wake me up at eleven o'clock", I asked Trina?

When I walked into the room he stood up, looking at me and talking, so I took him out his crib and laid him in the bed with me. He was sleepy, but he had some things he had to tell me. Soon he was asleep and I was falling right along with him. By eight o'clock both of us were asleep.

I drove back down the parkway, I got to work a little late, work seemed to pass by pretty quick, probably because I was thinking about the day that had just past, along with planning to do it again soon. I didn't want to hurry things at all, but I had enjoyed the day. Work was actually quiet, nothing was going on this night, I did my rounds and talked with the guys off and on through the night. I was still glad when seven o'clock came around and it was time to head for home. As I walked to my car after saying see ya to everybody, I thought about the breakfast that would be waiting for me that Mommy would have cooked. Of course I'd tell her and Pop about yesterday. There wasn't much traffic at all going the direction I was driving, so I enjoyed looking at the trees and watching for deer as I listened to the radio as I drove home. Half an hour later I was pulling up in the driveway, I could see all the blinds and shades were open at the house, which meant "I'm up". This was the first thing my parents did when they came downstairs in the morning, so of course that's what we had learned to do also. I pulled up to my parking space next to my porch, and headed for my parent's back door, as I walked into the kitchen Taz still in her pajamas was just coming into the kitchen we all exchanged kisses. Pop was just getting a plate to put the food on that was coming off the stove and out of the oven. After he put the plate near my mother he returned to his usual place at the kitchen table, Mom was scrambling eggs while Taz took some cups out of the cabinet. I walked over to the counter and filled the cups with hot coffee. Caffeine is supposed to keep people awake-not me, it doesn't seem to have any affect on keeping me stimulated, so drinking a cup or two wouldn't stop me from getting my eight hours of solid sleep. Mommy brought the large bowls with the cooked food to the table one with eggs and the other with sausage, she left the biscuits on the stove that way they'd stay warm. She knew each one of us would go back to get a second biscuit, that was a given, because she made the best biscuits everyone always said. My Pop was no slouch either when it came to biscuit making. Then again he could cook just about anything. Over breakfast we ate and I told them about my day with

Trina and Little Allen. They were excited for me. For one thing I knew they wanted them to come back. Mom and Trina got along so well, most people that saw them thought Trina was my Mother's daughter, and Taz thought Trina was one of the greatest playmates she had, and she always had my son calling herself keeping an eye on him. My Pop was the one to always give a caution sign to what ever you wanted to do. So he told me to be sure I was ready for them to come back, don't jump at something you're not 100% sure about and make sure you know the reason why you're sure or the reason why you're not sure. So after we all had eaten breakfast I headed out the back door for my crib, to be specific, heading to my bed. I started taking my shirt off, almost as soon as I entered the door, by the time I had gotten to the foot of the stairs I started pulling my undershirt off. What Pop had said ran across my mind as I started up the stairs to my bedroom. I didn't have to bother to set my alarm clock, because I was off today, but I sat the alarm so I wouldn't sleep the day away, I didn't want to miss this whole day, it was already pretty outside and the beginning of spring. There was nothing special going on this day, like I said just the beginning of spring, you know people stirring around a lot after the winter's over around here. I figured I'd get up a little after noon, didn't need to get my full eight hours of sleep right now, I could take a nap later today. Man, with the passing of each minute the desire to lay my head down on my pillow got stronger and stronger.

I was sleeping really good, when my telephone rang, I just tried to ignore it, I wasn't ready to wake up yet. Finally, I rolled over to answer the screaming phone, it was Marie on the line. She wanted to know what my plans were for tonight. I told her I didn't have any plans, and asked her why she wanted to know. Well, she was thinking about going out and wanted to know I felt like hanging with her. Sure that sounds good. "Dig this," I told her and began telling her about yesterday. After about ten minutes on the telephone she said she'd be over Momma's and Poppa's later this evening and she'd see me then. I hung the phone back on the receiver and thought about getting some more shut eye, but the alarm clock went off. I hit the snooze button and napped another ten minutes, the alarm sounded off again, I hit the snooze for the second time, the third time it sounded off I got up, so I could check out what might be going on around town. After I made it down the stairs, I headed straight for the stereo, some music would always get me going. "Get up the get down, get up outta yo seat", I was singing along with the Dramatics, when a knock at my door came. I peeped out the living room window to see who was at the door, it was Dave. I opened the door and told him to come on in make himself at home, like he usually did. Dave walked over to the kitchen table and sat down a brown paper bag, then he reached in it and pulled out some scotch. I went in the freezer to pull out an ice tray and grabbed two glasses from the dish drainer on the sink, I also picked up my bottle of wine. He fixed his drink and I poured a glass of wine, I took a sip then told him to come on outside on the porch. We drank, bullshitted and listened to music, until I thought I" better go and take my shower. I had come out and threw on a clean pair of jeans, and of course, freshened my drink. Dave was in the living room dancing to the O'Jays. I told him ,"Come on let's hit the street for a while. I have to be back around seven for a nap and to get ready to go out with Marie."

While we were out Dave and I stopped by his house to get a change of clothes for later tonight. No doubt he'd be out with us.

Dave had pretty much accepted that he and Laura had split up, although it had only been a few months. He didn't speak of trying to make the marriage work, he just visited his son on a regular. After leaving his place we hit the courts, just to check to see what was going on. There were a few guys there, no real game going down. So we shot a few, mostly a game of horse, then we played a half court game to twenty-one. From here we rode down the avenue, a lot of people were out, driving and strolling on the ave. We saw some guys we knew and pulled over to talk and shoot the breeze for a few. They said they were stopping in the Orchard Lounge for a drink after work, so I parked the car and we went on in with them. There were a few people in there, sitting around the bar, even had three women on the dance floor. I ordered my drink, took two sips and joined the chicks on the dance floor. Sometimes it's nice to go in a bar and it's almost empty. You know, like you have the place to yourself. We hung in there for close to an hour, before we went back to my crib to take a little nap and get ready for Marie. During the day, I had mentioned to Dave I was thinking about moving down by the beach. Didn't know when, but it had crossed my mind.

Later this night I was just waking up to get ready to go out when my phone rang,
I answered it was Debbi. I told her I was going out with my sister, but I could get with her the next day, so we made plans. As time went on, I realized Trina really meant what she had said, she was giving me time to get whatever it was in my system out of my system. I started seeing more of Debbi, until we became an item. About three months later, she moved in with me. We stayed at the house behind my parents' for some time. Debbi and I decided she'd move in with me since Trina and I hadn't fixed our relationship, to be honest, I wasn't doing anything to fix

our relationship either. It may have seemed easier to move on, so I tried to go on with my life. Debbi and I had good times, but I was drinking a lot more often, and taking out frustrations on her. Which she actually didn't deserve or maybe in some way she did, she was bold enough to walk into the house my wife and baby lived in.

My folks were getting tired of the mess going on at my place, so Debbi and I had packed the house up to move this upcoming weekend.

Junie............

I'd just about given up going to bars and clubs unless I took Paula. We went to parties or friends and family functions a lot though. Paula hadn't started to show much yet, if you looked close you could see her stomach starting to rise. So she was still looking forward to being in the hair show. The show was in three weeks, I had over heard her telling my cousin Les' wife Vaya. Vaya wanted to buy tickets to the show, of course Paula had some tickets handy in case someone wanted to buy a few. Vaya asked if Allen's wife was still going to be in the show. "Yes", Paula said, "she talked to Marie the other day. Trina's coming down this weekend."

Les and I walked downstairs to his basement, that's where all the fun stuff was. He put on some Sly and the Family Stone and then got us a beer from the refrigerator. We were sitting down at the bar when we heard the doorbell ring. It sounded like our cousin Jake and his wife Lydia, Vaya and Paula greeted them, then they all joined us downstairs. Where we all had a drink before we took some of the liquor and mixes upstairs to the main floor in the living and dining room areas. They had a hi-fi in the living room too, so Jake went down and came back with an arm full of records, so we could get this party started, and that's what we did. Vaya and Paula liked wine, I enjoyed wine, but don't get me wrong I really enjoyed a good stiff drink once in a while too. So we had a drink, then dancing and talking was going on. Paula was drinking a glass of juice, like a good mom-to-be. As usual my folks got together and hung out often and anybody there was always guaranteed a lot of laughs, talking about things we'd done and something funny would always happen when we were together. Man about midnight Paula and I made it out of Les' and Vaya's place, as usual everybody had a good time. I mean it wasn't a bunch of people just the three couples and Les' and Vaya's kids were upstairs, most of the time while we were there.

Paula had been having symptoms of being pregnant, a slight queasy feeling in the stomach that would come and go, even some smells made her nauseous. Poor little thing, she even had to take a nap every day, because she was sleepy most of the time.

Time had been going by pretty fast, finally this Saturday coming was the hair and fashion show Marie was doing at the Convention Hall. Marie, Paula, Trina, Leya, and Desia had all agreed on the hair, make-up and clothes they would wear for the show.
Thursday Trina kept her word and came down, the women went to the Convention Hall for rehearsals. Paula had wanted me to stop by there to see them, I think she really meant so I could see her. You know strutting on the runway, I had time, but that was for the women, so I didn't stop in. I was going to shoot some ball with the guys, and too, I would see them do their thing this weekend.

I went to spend some time with my boys and get a break from work and homework, tomorrow I was working half a day, then my week of vacation started. Later that night when I came in, Paula told me about some of the events that had went on at practice, how these three women who were modeling had gotten into an argument, and how the outfit she was to wear in the show had gotten too tight on her. My Mom and Aunt Kate could sew so they did some alterations on her dress so it would fit right especially around Paula's stomach.

It was Thursday two days before the show so I went to drop off Paula's dress to be altered. When I got to Mom and Dad's, Allen was there too. He asked me what I was wearing to the show. I told him, not a suit, something jazzy, like a pair of olive green pants, with a cream colored thin turtleneck sweater, black belt, black shoes and beaded necklace, colors black, cream and olive green. He was wearing a funky leisure like suit, not quite navy blue. The four of us made arrangements to meet at the house that way could find each other in the crowd. Man, they were expecting to have a big turnout.

Friday during the day, some of our cousins from out of town had come into town by the time I had gotten home from work. I'm telling you some of those patients at work could and did wear your ass out, so I needed a nap before I got together with everybody. I ate some fruit, took a quick warm shower and laid across the bed, and fell asleep before I even realized it.

By the time I woke up Mommy had already called for us, to see if we were coming over or if some of my cousins should come to my place. Around seven-thirty that night Paula and I made it down the highway to my parents'.

With people coming to stay for the weekend, in a way our family was kind of hoping Trina and Little Allen would come and stay for the weekend. Figuring the more time her and my brother spent together, the more likely it would be that they'd get back together.

As the night went on we accepted that she and the baby weren't coming tonight.

After hanging out Paula and I back to our apartment around two in the morning. Saturday morning came around I called my mother to see what was going on. he told me, Trina had called there about fifteen minutes ago. She was calling from the train station and wanted somebody to pick her and the baby. Of course, Allen went to pick them up.

After I cooked breakfast and we had eaten, we just relaxed for a bit. Later, I got up and drove to the beach to go for a walk on the boardwalk. Meanwhile Paula stayed home, said she'd rest for a while longer, because the girls in the show had to meet at my sister's at two o'clock.

After I left the beach I stopped by my brother's place. A few of our cousin's were staying with him, because he had a two bedroom apartment. I sat down and talked for a little while, before I decided I'd better get back home for a nap myself. Paula had already gone to my sister's by the time I walked in the apartment.

Marie............

My brother Allen had lived in the house behind Momma and Poppa for two years, when he drank he was a different person and that caused friction between he and Papa, then him and Debbi fussing and fighting, there was too much of his business too close to the parents, you know. So they asked him to move and he was actually glad to move. He and Debbi moved to an apartment building not far from the ocean and just a block from the lake.

Monica and myself now lived in the house he had moved out of. We told you we were a close family.

Well, it was time to start getting ready for our hair show, it was good I had moved, I had more space here to spread out all the things we'd need for the show and setting up hair dryers and things like that.

"Okay Leya let me start with your head first, you have that super fine hair, that might need a little extra", Marie said.

"A little extra what", Leya asked.

"You know your hair, a little extra anything and everything", Marie replied.

Leya had already washed and set her hair. She and I both went to beautician school together. I was fantastic with chemicals on hair and she was super with haircuts.

I had told her the other day to set her hair with beer that would make it hold better and it's a great conditioner, because of the protein. She had done as I told her, so her hair wasn't hard to work with, I just applied quite a bit of hair spray to keep it in place. First of all by the time we stopped running our mouths and eating, it was already three thirty, that brought us to four fifteen and I had three more heads to style. Every thing they were wearing could be put on without messing up their hair and make-up. I moved on to Desia's hair, Leya had cut Desia's hair short. It was black shiny, short and sassy. I styled it with a full crown and it tapered real quick and the nape of her neck. I moved on through hairstyles with an ease, styling, spraying and gelling. Paula had a sharp shag, with a bang. Pumped and teased at the top to be more dramatic. Trina had real healthy looking black hair, but I had styled dark brown wig with highlights to bring out her eyes and fantastic features. I finally got myself together last, but not least.

Six o'clock we headed for the Convention Center, that's where the show was going on later. We joined a bunch of other women and men that were getting ready for the show. Once we arrived, we got dressed and there were a few make-up artists there to help put make-up on everybody. It had to be applied very heavily so it would show up on stage with the bright lights.

I enjoyed the excitement that came along with these shows, the lights, the music, people running all over backstage, the overdone hair and clothes, the hum and vibe from the audience. Before we realized it the seats and tables were almost filled up and the show was about to begin. One of the partners named Anthony, that had asked me about being in his show came over to speak with me. So I'm thinking he's just going to talk to me about something pertaining to the show, which he did mention, but he wanted to talk to me in privacy tomorrow. I agreed to meet him for lunch. As the night went on I kind of felt he was keeping an eye on me a bit more than the other models and stylists. And yes, I played up to it a tiny bit, enough to interest him, but not enough to be obvious. You know how we do. Besides out front my boyfriend was there. After all the strutting around on stage and back stage, we went out to mingle with the guests. I walked over to my brother Allen, I told him, that he and Junie looked so cool. I went and gave Marvin a kiss, I hadn't seen him in two weeks. Just as I stepped back to let him check me out up close, Anthony joined us, saying he didn't mean to interrupt, but he just wanted to thank me and my models for doing such a great job. Anthony spoke to each one of us, while talking to me and the models, Marv went to the bar to get me a drink. When he returned and handed me my screwdriver cocktail, it almost seemed like he did it to get my attention. I acknowledged him and thanked him as we continued to talk, the group of us. Then Anthony excused his self and continued to mingle with everyone he came across. The music had gotten some people on the dance floor. I went to dance with my cousin that was visiting from Baltimore, we were doing our thing. Afterwards, we returned to the area of tables our group was setting at, they were having a good time we could tell because the laughter was loud. I'd say it was about half and hour later, when I made it to the dance floor again, with another cousin, when Anthony showed up dancing with some nice looking girl next to us. After two songs he asked me to dance and hey I did. He was fine, I was having a good time and wasn't hurting anybody. As we were dancing he'd place his hand on my waist. I felt another hand slide around my waist starting from my back and sliding around me to the side of my stomach, it was Marv. He asked Anthony if he could cut in. Anthony was like sure and flashed a big bright smile. As Marv and I danced I glanced Anthony checking me out every now and then while I was on the floor and I began to think Marv was checking him, checking me.

Marv mentioned to me that Anthony seemed to be interested in me. I was telling him, "Yeah, he really seems to like my work" Marv was like, "It's more than your work he's interested in."

"Stop it sweetie", I told him. "Now go on and keep shakin' your ass for me", I said to him. He just laughed and spun around in front of me and he really did shake that cute ass to the music for me, and I reciprocated for him. Now I could feel Anthony watching and somehow I picked up on his feeling of not liking what he'd just seen.

I acknowledged to myself that he was attracted to me now. And no I hadn't told Marv about the lunch meeting I have with Anthony set for tomorrow. I'd figure that one out by tomorrow morning. Really, I don't know what this guy wanted to speak with me about. I did tell Leya and my mother about the meeting.

Don't get me wrong, I'm independent and I do what I want. I just don't want to hear no mouth from Marv, and don't want no pouting or attitude. He's good for pouting.

As the night went on we were having a really nice time and mingling. While Marv and I were dancing, Anthony had gotten behind me on the dance floor, we all were working up a nice little sweat out there. As the one song ended Marvin left the dance floor and went to our table. That's when Anthony got too close for comfort, he had his back to me, his butt had rubbed up against mine. Not on purpose I think, just a crowded dance floor, you know.

Then a minute later I felt his front rub up against me, for a split second, again a crowded dance floor. I turned his way and danced for a minute, then back to the other guy I was dancing with. There were some people that had joined the groovin'. Now this time as we danced he bumped me, but this time I felt something hard rub up against me. I felt his hardness for a second or two, before I realized or admitted what it was. I moved a way from him a bit, not making any notice of what had just happened. The next song came on and we continued to dance when I felt him rub it across my hip, he was doing this on purpose, I knew now. I made an excuse to leave the floor and as I was headed for our table Marv was approaching me looking unhappy. I thought to myself, "Oh shit, it's about to be on in here. Please not now."

Marv said he was ready to go, I just said that was fine and I was tired myself. We went to tell our people we'd catch them in the morning. I didn't dare ask him why he wanted to leave, that would allow a can of worms to get loose. We walked to his Cadillac in silence. The sky was pitch black and the stars were so bright. Once inside the car I started to try to say a few words. Thanking him for coming and being so supportive. He at the same time was telling me how much fun he'd had and that we looked like pros up on stage.

When we arrived home I was so glad to be there, I was really tired and a little tipsy from those drinks. I'd had quite a few of them. Monica was at my Uncle's for the night, that was good. I was tired but not so tired Marv and I didn't get it on. Anyway the next morning came, by the time we stirred out of bed it was close to eleven o'clock. Marv said, "I have some bad news."

I guess the look on my face looked too upset. He said, "Not bad like that, I have to leave in about an hour or so. Got to get back to Boston today, but I couldn't miss the show last night. Is that okay with you?"

I was like, "You are just the sweetest man I've ever seen. You came all the way down here just for that. I would have understood if you hadn't came," I told him.

I cooked breakfast and made some coffee. I wasn't a coffee drinker so I made enough for him and I had orange juice with my food. We both were eating like we were starving, shit I felt like I was starving. I had made a large breakfast, just as we were finishing up our plates, a cousin came down the stairs to go to the bathroom. My cousins had stayed out later than Marv and I, he looked like he was worn out and hung over. Good mornings were exchanged and when Jay came out the bathroom he got a plate and a cup of coffee and joined us at the table. We talked about the night before, how much fun we'd had and how hard Jay had partied. Around noon Marv excused himself from the table and went back upstairs to get his things.

When he came back down, I walked him out to his car, gave him a kiss and told him to call me when he got home, that way I'd know if he arrived home safely.

I walked back in my place and told Jay I had an appointment this afternoon, actually in a short while and to help himself and I'd be getting ready for this meeting. I couldn't believe things had worked out the way they did. I didn't have to tell Marv about this lunch meeting, there's nothing more to this than business. Anthony had just had too much to drink last night. Then I thought to myself, maybe I should get a drink before I met with Anthony, you know a little something to loosen me up. While Jay was talking to me and another cousin who had entered the kitchen, I then went into my walk in pantry to get a bottle of vodka I had on the shelf, to mix with some orange juice. Anybody that came to my house knew to make themselves at home, so they were moving about the down stairs getting breakfast and talking. As I entered the den I turned on the stereo, and put on an album, a little something a bit mellow, to help ease us into the upcoming day. With my folks, a night of partying would turn into a weekend of partying, for sure. Not that we had anything special to do this day, but after partying last night, some relaxing music to give you a little groove, but keep you feeling kind of low keyed. I called to my cousin Jay who was at the kitchen table, "Here's something to help you with your." Before I could even finish my sentence he called back to me, "I don't have no hangover."

"Who said anything about a hangover. But since you said it, here's something for those that might have a slight hangover," I called back to him. I had to finish my sentence because they were laughing at us going back and forth, it was so evident boyfriend had tied one on last night and was paying for it this morning. I went on up the stairs to get myself together. I'd wear this jumpsuit my mother had picked up for me.

An hour later I was dressed and ready to go, so I called for a cab to pick me up and take me to the restaurant to meet with Anthony. I walked down the driveway to the waiting car with a yard of family almost accompanying me to the taxi, I got in and rode to Belmar, where on the dock they had great seafood, fresh off the boat. The boats literally stopped at the back door of the restaurants and unloaded today's catch.

I had arrived about fifteen minutes early, this way it would give me time to get myself together and watch him make his way to our table. As he appeared through the people that were near the door waiting for a table, he stood out. He was tall and fine. A low haircut that was silky and curly, he had on a crew cut neck shirt that fit very close. It was cream colored with navy blue slacks. I put out my hand as he approached me for a handshake. He took my hand but didn't shake it, he touched his pretty lips to my hand in a gentlemanly kiss, then he seated himself across from me. We ordered drinks and talked about the show and hairstyles. As we ate our seafood platters, we talked and laughed so easily together. The conversation just seemed to flow from one topic to another. He asked if I had ever thought about doing shows as a profession. I answered "No, the opportunity had never presented itself."

As we talked he asked me to do hair for a show that was to take place in Philadelphia. I almost jumped across the table at getting this chance, but I played it cool. I told him that sounds good and would like the details about the show. He told me what he knew at the time and would talk with me on a regular to keep me on top of things. As we neared the end of our meal I asked him if it would be possible for him to drop me off. He was like, "No problem, I'd be glad to."

He was looking at me a bit too much, yet not quite enough to make me self-conscious of his eyes watching but, I was very aware of his eyes on me. On our way out the restaurant to the car he put his hand on my lower back to usher me towards the door and towards his car.

And yes it felt good there, kind of like it belonged there. Just a nice guy with a good opportunity for me, I thought to myself and let's leave it at that. Anthony opened the car door so I could get in, then he walked around to his side of the car. I gave him driving directions as he drove me home. When we arrived in front of my door, most of our visitors had left for home. I figured I'd be nice and I invited him in. He was like, "Sure, let me park."

As we walked up the steps and walkway to my parents' front porch, my mother and cousin, along with my Aunt Kate were setting out there. I told him to have a seat, while I went to get a cool drink of lemonade for him. By the time I came to the porch, my father and cousin from Baltimore had joined them on the porch. His conversation flowed easily with my folks, we all laughed and talked about a little of everything. After about twenty minutes or so, Anthony decided it was time for him to leave, so I walked him down to his car. When we reached his car we exchanged farewells and he kissed me on my cheek, then got in his car and pulled off. I went back to the porch, my mother was smiling and teasing, "I saw him kissing on you."

I said, "Momma that was just a simple friendly kiss. He seems like a nice guy. That's all there was to it."

I excused myself and called Monica from a neighbor's yard to come in the house with me for a while. She was out there playing with my little sister Taz and the little girl next door Mary. Monica, Mary and Taz came inside, we ate some watermelon and watched television for a short while, before the k ids headed outside, I told Monica to stay in the yard, I'd be calling her in to get ready for bed soon. I didn't have to worry, because nine out of ten times she was playing in our yard or right next door. The girls went back outside and I gradually fell asleep on the sofa trying to watch the Mod Squad.

I had been asleep for about an hour I guess, when I awoke to the telephone ringing. I got up and went into the kitchen to answer the phone, it was Marvin. I told him to hold on while I checked on Monica inside. I was glad to hear his voice, we were talking for about fifteen minutes, then he started telling me he wasn't going to be able to make it down this coming weekend. I offered to come up his way and bring Monica with me. He said it wasn't a good idea, he had quite a bit of running around he'd be doing. Look, to me I felt like he just didn't want us to come up to his place. He could take care of his business and whenever he got back to the house we'd meet him there.

That wasn't good enough. So I though to myself, I'm not going to force myself on him.

So I said, "That's alright I understand. I don't want to force myself on you. I'll see you the following weekend then." He was like, "That's solid."

Close to forty-five minutes later we hung up. I walked to the living room door to see what the girls were doing, they were coming onto the porch towards me.

"Mommy said dinner's ready", Taz told me.

Then she opened the door and asked what's wrong. She was very observant, had always been. I told her I had just talked with Marvin and he pissed me off a bit.

She told me not to worry it'll be okay as she leaned her sweaty little head on my breasts and hugged me.

I told them to come let's go eat. I figured I'd just make my plate, so I could set in front of the television and have a screwdriver with my dinner. I'd had one before I fell asleep and hadn't finished it.

Before I could get in my folks' kitchen, our neighbors came around over bringing a big pot or red rice and beans. One of my cousins was still here and was leaving tomorrow morning, so all talked while we enjoyed our meal.

Early Sunday afternoon most of our visitors headed back to their homes. Although I had enjoyed everybody, it was going to be good to hear peace and quiet again.

After we'd eaten and cleaned up I returned home to lounged on my lounge chair while Monica was upstairs watching television and reading before bedtime. Everything was quiet again and everyone seemed to relax and rest getting ready to face the upcoming workweek.

On Monday I spoke with Anthony and now here it was half way through the week one evening, I had freshened my drink and was more than half way finished nibbling on my dinner when the phone rang again. To my surprise, I heard a pleasant voice on the other end full of an Italian accent.

"Hello Darlin', Anthony said.

"It's so nice to hear your voice. How is everything", I asked?

"Oh, believe me things would be so much better if I had you here with me, helping out. I've been running like mad. I have an update of information about our tour and I was wondering if you might want to meet me for a weekend or if you'd prefer I could come get you. Look all I know is I need a break, total relaxation for a few days", he said.

I replied back at him, "I can just imagine that much traveling and working non-stop, you deserve a break."

"But you haven't answered my question. I want to spend the weekend with you, do you want to meet me or should I pick you up. Is the question", Anthony asked me.

"Well, I'd probably enjoy spending a weekend with you, but I'll have to take a rain check on it. You know I am seeing someone, although it seems to have come to a stand still", I answered.

"It's not like we haven't spent time together before. What's the deal? Talk to me, don't let me make a fool of myself", Anthony said.

"Look, there's no way you're making a fool of yourself I just need to see what is going on for sure with my dying relationship. I truly enjoyed talking with you", I told him. "Hey, I guess I understand, but to be honest I'm not happy with your answer. Then on the other hand I respect what you're trying to do, even if it makes little sense to me. I wanted to explain the business to you and leisurely go over plans for the Philadelphia show", Anthony replied.

"Sweetie, I'm going to have to call you back tonight. If it's alright with you", he asked?

"I'll be here with the phone in my hand", I said laughing.

"Oh, what's the joke. Tell me, I dare you to tell me", he said pretending to be serious, but I could hear the laughter in his voice.

I told him to call me when he got a chance tonight. It was summer and I wasn't working at the school during the day, just doing hair, so I could sleep late if I were up late.

Now to be honest, I go to bed almost when the sun went down, except in the summer, sometimes I'd go to sleep before the sun went down. A girl's got to get her beauty rest. I thought to myself I'll call Marv tomorrow to see what was really going on with him. My Aunt Kate came in the door, a few minutes later my mother and Monica walked in the door, Monica got ready for bed, while my mother, Aunt Kate and I talked our girl talk, we always had so much fun together. We were doing our girl talk when my telephone rang again. Leya had been over earlier during the day, so I didn't think she'd be calling. Monica answered the telephone, while standing over near the stove. She was smiling when she called me to the phone. It was Marv, we spoke for about five minutes, then I asked him if I could call him back in a little while I had a few friends over. He wanted to know what friends were at my place, I wanted him to think I really had a few guests over, not family as usual. I said back, "You don't know them, but you'll have to meet them one day soon."

"Marie, well what are their names," Marv asked.

Marv, come on why? That still wouldn't make you know them. They'll be leaving in about an hour. We have to talk about us not seeing each other often enough, with your lame ass excuses," I told him.

He was like, "Girl what are you talking about. I know I've been busy these days, but if it'll make you feel better or more at ease, we can talk until the sun comes up," he told me.

I thought to myself he can be so full of shit, and it seemed like he was getting more and more full of it. I just said, "I'll call you back in a few."

I returned to my kitchen table where Mama and Aunt Kate were eating honeydew melon. I asked them if they had heard that? They(men) are something else, was the look they both gave me. I told them a bit more about the story of what was going on. I tried to give Marv the benefit of the doubt, you know with him running a prostitution house. He was still a father and a grandfather, he tried to do the boyfriend thing right, but it seemed to just be his way. Being a player, was in his nature, a big baller.

Monica had come out of the bathroom and put on a clean pair of pajamas.

Mommy said, "Let's ride down the avenue and see what's going on."

We always got excited over doing this, we did it once or twice a week. Riding down the avenue, just looking at people act a fool and trying to be cool, from there we'd proceed down to ride by the boardwalk, to see all the people down there. We'd see some of the stupidest, and funniest stuff going on. Sometimes we'd be almost hysterical with laughter or just entertained.

I told Monica, "Put on your flipflops, and go tell Taz to come on and don't forget to get Mama and Aunt Kate's pocketbooks."

The girl was gone in a flash across the yard. While she went to do that, us older girls, made our way out to my mom's Oldsmobile Taz and Monica came out the door with the pocketbooks, Taz locked the back door and off we went.

While we were riding I have to admit I was thinking about Marv and Anthony. I had a little history with Marv and I was thinking if I thought there was a chance of a satisfying future with him, I wouldn't even consider another man, but somewhere inside I must have known this wasn't really about to happen. He had asked me to move to Boston with him, but his business wasn't really a good environment for my daughter and to be honest me either.

Then at the same time Marv's a nice guy, just not quite legitimate. Then I tried to consider all Anthony had to offer, and leave out the fact that he was so fine. Weighing things out Anthony would win, because of how he made his living, the honest way, not on the verge of being illegal. But then there was one major problem here, Anthony hadn't asked me and my daughter to come live with him and he sure hadn't said anything about marriage. While I was doing all this thinking, I realized someone was talking to me – "What did you say Aunt Kate? My mind was a thousand miles away for a few minutes."

Aunt Kate repeated what she had said. After I answered her, I went back to thinking about Anthony and Marvin. I decided all I could do was play things by ear.

Usually Marv and I called each other almost every night, so after I got home I was expecting my telephone to ring, but as time went on, I realized he wasn't calling me tonight. To be honest it stung me a bit, but then I remembered I'd told him I call him. Hell, he had excuses not to come visit and for me not to come to his place.

Meanwhile, Monica had taken her bath before we went for our ride and had now gone to lay in her bed and watch television as soon as we got in from riding. I checked to make sure she was asleep then I went in my pantry to get a glass and a shot of vodka then in the fridge to get some ice cold orange juice. I made myself a cold screwdriver on the rocks, took two or three sips, then I placed it in the refrigerator. Before settling down to relax and enjoy my drink I took me a luke water bath, after finishing my quick bath, I got my drink out the refrigerator, and went to my room, turned my television on and put the fan on low, then I got into my bed that seemed to feel extra good tonight. It seemed like I'd had a long day. I'd taken a sip from my glass when the phone rang. It kind of startled me, my first thought uhm it's Marvin, I answered it, it wasn't Marvin.

Instead it was Leya calling to run her mouth for a few minutes. I finished my drink while I was on the telephone with her, turned my television off and slept like a baby. I always woke up before the sun arose, so I'd done my housework by ten o'clock. Leya came over around eleven, Dave showed up around noon and we were sitting on the porch with my stereo playing, having cocktails and laughing our asses off, when a Cadillac pulled up in the driveway.

We recognized the car right away, it was Marvin. I sure was not expecting to see him, man, I played it cool as hell. I stood up with my short shorts on and my tube top with my drink in my hand and I strutted over to his car. We hugged and gave a nice but brief kiss before he greeted the others. By now my parents had come into their backyard, which was my front yard. We all hung out on the porch for a while. I went inside to my kitchen, hoping Marv would follow me and he did. I told him I wanted to talk to him before the day was over, afterwards we went back outside and continued to socialize for a while longer. It wasn't too long after we'd gone back out to the porch when my company had drifted home. Monica was now on my parent's front porch, so Marvin and I sat on my porch and we discussed what was going on with him and us. I got some answers but, still had questions that I didn't feel satisfied with the answer I had gotten, but somehow he really couldn't answer them. So I finally came out and asked, "Should we start seeing other people?" His nostrils flared, "Where the fuck did that idea come from" he asked?

"You can't answer some questions and I don't want you to feel as though you're being put on the spot. I'm trying to make it easy for you", I stated.

"Do you want to see somebody else" he asked me?

I told him to be honest, "I feel as though you don't have time or want to make time for me."

"Yeah, it's hard to be in two places at once sometimes, and yes sometimes I can't make it down here, and yes again, I don't ask you to come up there too much, because I feel as though I wouldn't be doing right to have you up there then I'm busy", he told me.

"You wouldn't have to entertain me, but I do miss you at times", I told him.

He then went on to say, "Well if I remember correctly, I asked you to come live with me. You're the one that said no."

I've never just lived with a man, and I do have a daughter to consider", I said.

"Well baby, I ain't ready for no marriage. Been there, done that jive and ain't in no hurry to hang myself again", he threw out of his mouth.

"I don't want to live with a man, but I also want to be sure before or if I remarry. That's why I said no. Not because I don't have feelings for you. You know what I mean", I told him.

"Yeah I know what you mean. You're gonna get you some nigga that's ready to get married", he said.

"That's not what I meant and you know it", I told him.

"I can't believe I came down here to hear this mess. Let's take a break and relax for a while", Marvin said.

And so we did. He walked over to visit my family, I went inside and called Leya.

Then I laid out on my lounge chair, with the fan setting in the window, it was so nice and cool in here. He came back in my house about an hour later, he asked if I wanted to go for a ride, I told him, "Sure why not. I'll let my mother know as we back out the driveway."

As he and I rode around listening to music and talking, we both seemed to feel more at ease, on the way back home he mentioned about going out for drinks later or cooking out. He was always down for entertaining, because he liked to be seen. So he dropped me off then he went to the store to buy liquor, mixers and steaks for the grill. While he was gone I put my stereo speakers out on the porch and let the grill for the charcoal to get ready. I called Leya to come over and bring a date, my friend Desia had moved to North Carolina or else I'd have called her over too. As soon as the family heard music coming from their backyard, Taz and Monica came around to see what was going on. Then my father came and he checked the charcoal, then he went in his house. Meanwhile Monica, Mary, and Taz who was an excellent dancer got to dancing, so I joined in. We did the three way bump for a few minutes, before Aunt Kate and Momma came dancing into the backyard. By this time Marv pulled up in the driveway, so me and the kids helped take the bags out the back seat and take them into the house. When I came back outside, which was only about five minutes later, Leya and Ty had walked up the driveway. They all were laughing and talking in the yard. Another good friend, Rosa, which my mother knew from them working in a sewing factory together(Mary's mom) came over, she said she had cooked a pot of red rice and beans, she could bring it over. Well, we love red rice and beans, so we were like "Yeah bring that shit on."

My brother Allen pulled in the driveway. Poppa came out with some homemade peppers, I ran inside and threw together a salad and took some chicken out of my freezer. I gave the meat to Monica to take to Poppa, he was the grill master, as usual. We had a ball this evening, it just always happened like this, people just getting together at any time for no reason. Next thing you know my Uncle J showed up, yes our own personal Sammy Davis Jr. was on the scene.

About eleven- thirty we all parted for the night. That night Marv and I made love like we had never had a problem or discussion and then slept like we'd been sedated. Morning came and we could again feel there was something in the air between us.

We'd had so much fun yesterday, we had forgotten about this stump in our relationship. He was lying on the sofa, when Monica came in from my parent's house. She spent the night there sometimes on the weekend. She'd call out the window from Taz's bedroom window, "Good night Mommy," and I'd call back to her, "Good night Sugar face."

She sat on the lounge chair with me watching television, then I made my baby some lunch and told her to go get her spelling book so we could read for a while. After reading for half an hour she was ready and rested up to play kickball with the kids, in the yard next door. After she went out to play, I said to Marv we still have to see what exactly is going on between us or is everything fixed now. He said it's fixed, and let's leave it that way.

Well, you can't have a conversation by yourself so I left it for now. That evening Marvin left headed home back to Boston.

A few days after Marvin had left, Anthony called to tell me he'd be in town and wanted to see me.

So a week and a half past I had called Marvin several times, most times he returned my calls and he did call me back, but not the way he used to. Two and a half weeks had now past, during this time I heard from Marv, but he seemed somewhat distant. I said to myself, leave it alone and do what you have to. He did say he'd be down to see me in a few weeks.

Later during the week he called and during our conversation said he wouldn't be able to make it. I thought to myself now it's been a month since I last saw him, and I've offered to come to his place.

A few days later Anthony called, to confirm us getting together. I told him that would still be great.

So when that fourth week came and Marv had a reason he couldn't have me come to his place, I brought the same stuff up again. "Look what's up, you're so busy?"

"Nothing is up, baby", he said, "I'll be down there next week."

I told him next week wasn't a good time for him to come down. Of course he wanted to know why not. I just told him I had quite a bit going on that week, the following week would be better. At this minute I wasn't caring if I didn't see him for another four months. Now that I was busy and things weren't at his convenience, he wanted to be persistent about coming to see me. I stuck to my guns and told him I'd be busy that week.

I thought to myself what if I was having a good time with Anthony and he and I decided he should stay a day or two. Shit Marv was playing games and I had been patient, now it was time I turned the tables on him. I don't mean playing with him, but backing up away from him. Before Marvin and I hung up the phone, I had a slight sad feeling, but glad that I hadn't made everything to his convenience. As for Marv he was aggravated, but I didn't really care anyway.

"Don't do me any favors Marvin, if you have any problems or just don't want to come down then don't. It's no skin off my back. Maybe on second thought maybe, you shouldn't come down", I told the son of a bitch.

"Solid", that was all he said to what I'd said. Then he had the nerve to say he had to hang up now.

Just think, at one time I thought I was falling in love with this nigger, but maybe I wasn't falling in love or could it be something had caused me to stop falling in love with him.

I put the phone on the cradle after he'd hung up then went to make me a screwdriver. As I headed for the bathroom to run water to take a relaxing bath my telephone ran again. It was the woman I worked for in her beauty salon, she asked me about helping find some pictures of hairstyles to hang on the salon walls. I told her have my little sister could draw some pictures for the salon. She was glad we were able to settle that request instantly. The next day I asked Taz to draw three or four pictures for the salon, she was happy to help out, she was very artistic. She drew three pictures, one of a short hairstyle, one almost shoulder length, and the last one was of a long hair style. The pictures were perfect, so I took them to the shop (hair salon) and Mrs. Cotton the salon owner and my co-workers were so impressed, because my sister was only twelve years old. I was half way through my workday when Anthony crossed my mind.

Then Leya walked in the salon, she was expecting a customer in half an hour. Leya had brought in a box of donuts for the hairdressers, so she put the box in the back room, which was closed to customers.

I finished setting my customer's hair then placed her under the dryer and set the timer. I couldn't wait to get back there to those donuts. Two glazed donuts and a half-cup of coffee disappeared into my mouth. I thought to myself, I'd give Anthony a call tonight. He had backed off, because of my relationship I was guessing. The work day finally came to an end. My Momma, Monica and Taz were out in the car waiting for me.

Leya had gotten a Volkswagen Beetle, so I rode with her most days, but she had only a few appointments today, so she had come to work later than me.

Before getting in my mother's car, I went across the street to the liquor store to get some vodka, orange juice and pork skins, before I got in the car and it had started to sprinkle. We all laughed and talked on the way home. We pulled up into the driveway, Momma went home, Monica and Taz came to my place. They went into the living room and turned on the television, I went straight to the bathroom to relieve myself and wash my face. Then I went to the sink and mixed my cocktail. I had already precooked dinner last night, so I put it on the stove to heat up and told the kids to clean up for dinner. Afterwards, they went into the pantry to get dishes for us to eat with. I had made chilli with rice on the side and had a big box of Ritz crackers to go with it. I made a bowl for Poppa and sent Monica to take it to him. Taz got the Kool-aid out the refrigerator and put in on the kitchen table. As soon as Mo got back we fixed our bowls and went in the living room to eat and watch television.

We'd just finished up dinner when my door opened, it was Marvin five weeks late. I'd given him a key a while ago. I was shocked as shit to see him, he wasn't looking happy like usual. I stood to give him a hug, but his hug back was emotionless. I sent the girls to my parent's house so Marv and I could talk. As they walked to the door I picked up my glass to sip my screwdriver, then offered him a cocktail. He asked for vodka on the rocks, so I fixed it for him. He drank his drink down in two gulps, then sat on the sofa, not next to me.

I attempted to make conversation even though there was tension in the air. He would responded with a snappy response or sarcasm. So I was like, "What's your problem? You drove five and a half hours to get here, to have an attitude. What's goin' on?"

He said, "You and I are having problems or is it just me."

I responded, "Yes we are having problems. I've been trying to address the problem for a few months, I left it alone, because I felt I was the only one working on it or even concerned. You've had reasons or excuses for us not to see each other most of the time, I let it slide as much as I could, then figured, fuck it, whatever happens happens."

"I'm busy, I own a business. You can't always come first", Marvin said.

I interrupted with, "You own a whore house. I didn't ask or expect to be the most important thing in your life, but why the distant attitude? If you don't want our relationship to grow say so. If you want to slow it way down, let me know. Do you want this engagement ring back? You know this ring you gave me to keep me quiet and buy you some time while you kept me hanging on. Want it back?"

He had the nerve to hold out his palm, like he wanted me to place it in his hand. I was looking at him like for real?

"Maybe that would be a good idea he said in a low voice almost like he regretted it. Then he said, "No keep it."

Then he just walked out the house and down the sidewalk, I was behind him asking questions, I was actually mad and hurt. We were about three houses from my driveway when he started talking shit and grabbed me by my arm. "Let go of me", I told him.

This fool was snatching me around when he dropped his keys. That's when he let go of my arm to try and pick up his keys, but it was almost dark out and I saw them first, so I picked them up. Before I could even straighten up good from picking up his keys, he was saying, "Give them here. Give me my keys."

So I said, "Wait a minute."

Then he started grabbing at me again. I yanked my arm out of his hand and threw those damned keys clean across the street into an overgrown lot of grass that had one huge tree setting on it. His ass got furious when I threw those keys. He ran over to the lot, looking in the direction he thought his keys had gone. There was no way he'd find them, so he gave up after a few minutes and stormed around the block to Dunkin Donuts, he ran into my brother Allen, as Allen was coming out of the liquor store. Marvin rode with my brother back to the lot where his keys were lost forever. Of course he had told Allen the story. They pulled up in front of the house. Allen came in the house laughing aloud, yet to himself. So Momma asked what's so funny. He told her about the incident, she joined in laughing. Then told me I shouldn't have thrown his keys over there. Then Allen said he was going out to shine his car lights on the lot to see if that might help. Mama and I looked out the living room window where we could see them out there across the street looking for the keys. No luck, the both of them gave up and came into the house after Allen parked his car. I was in my Mom's kitchen when Marvin came into the kitchen with a disgusted sigh leading his way. I had my back to him washing the plate I had dirtied. He walked over next to me and quietly asked, "Can I stay at your place over night. Maybe, tomorrow I'll have some luck looking for my keys."

Then he of course told me how messed it up was that I threw his keys like that. I just told him he could stay and walked into the living room. Good nights were being said when Papa came in the house, afterwards I got my daughter and went home. While Monica was getting ready for bed I fixed up the sofa bed for Marv. That nigga didn't know how lucky he was to even stay on my sofa.

Back when I was seeing this guy that was in the Army he did me wrong, made me mad or hurt. Really a combination of both of those feelings, hurt that made me mad. Anyway, I picked up a garbage can and threw it through the window of this guy's pretty little Corvette. I threw it so hard the garbage can landed on the gear shift in between the car seats. He knew he had done enough for me to react like that. So he didn't fight me, he shut his mouth and got out of my face Months later he asked me to marry him.

I think most men don't want a flunky, they want a nice lady, smart, a little dependent on him, strong-to represent him when he's not present, a whore in bed, but won't take too much shit from him or anybody else.

I finished making up the sofa bed then went upstairs to my bedroom. I really didn't want to be nice and let him stay here, I should have told him to sleep in his Cadillac. They have a reputation for be comfortable cars.

The next morning I woke up and went downstairs with my robe on, sponged off real quick then headed out the door to join my folks on the patio sipping coffee. Don't think for a minute my parents had or have the perfect marriage. They've had fights, I mean knock down fights, other women, but as Papa had gotten older he mellowed out.

Junie............

I pulled up in the driveway and got out the car, walked around my white Super Sport Chevelle, it was rimmed out. I opened the door for Paula she was looking very pregnant now. She was eating all the chocolate she could get her chubby little fingers on. I dropped her off at my parent's house when I had to go to work or school, because she was close to the due date. We really had around six weeks until the due date, but we figured better safe than sorry, plus she was happy here. You see, Paula's adoptive parents had disowned her when we decided to get married, so my family was all the family she basically had. But, today we were stopping by on our way to the beach, we'd stopped and gotten a dozen donuts to have with the folks. We had already eaten breakfast, but Paula was craving these donuts. Besides we'd pick up Taz and Monica and take them with us riding. I know Paula got tired of my little sister hanging out with us and now we even had my little niece with us sometimes, but I will say they're good kids and quite a bit of fun.

Sometimes when I had a girl over, before I got married I mean. Taz was about four years old, she'd be watching television and I'd make loud kissing noises because I knew that would get her attention. She'd whip her head around to see what was going on, then my date and I would snicker, because we'd get a kick out of teasing her. After she checked us out, she'd give the girl a look like, "you'd better stop it or else."

She was funny, one day my best friend kept playing and nagging her, then he picked her up by her feet had her hanging upside down, she yelled to him several times to, stop and leave me alone, but he just kept on at her. He was swinging her around, she got mad and grabbed her plastic bat while he was swinging her and started wearing his ass out with it, he'd grab the bat, then she'd kick him. He was yelling out for my mother to come get this kid.

Anyway, things were going good for Paula and myself. We were living in a nice one bedroom apartment with a big walk-in closet directly across from our bedroom. The closet is where we were going to put the baby's crib and dresser. No, don't even think that we'd close the closet door it would stay open, like it was part of our bedroom.

Allen............

Debbi and I had been having our good and bad times as most couples do. I didn't run the streets much, but I could be a pain in the butt when I drank. Debbi loved me so she put up with it and overlooked it. During this time I had decided she needed to learn to drive. I sometimes thought to myself, what was up with me the women I was involved with not knowing how to drive. Anyway, I'd taken her out for a few lessons, it was so funny, she drove like a little kid, she kept her hands and the steering wheel in constant motion. The car was never going in a straight line, just wiggling, it was unbelievable. I kept at her about that, because the car was just swaying down the street like a snake. After a few weeks of the swaying car not getting any better we both gave up on her learning how to drive. I couldn't dig that she wasn't getting any better, like the car not driving straight. After months of her not learning or getting much better, I gave up at teaching her. As time was passing, honestly, I'd started causing more and more arguments. I don't think I know why or to be honest maybe I knew of too many reasons why, but wasn't ready to admit them. Maybe, somewhere inside I was still feeling something like resenting Trina and my son not being with me? Was the drinking helping me to escape this or maybe it was a way of punishing myself. Well, Debbi kept bringing up marriage but, I wasn't even divorced yet. I was honest with Debbi when I told her I wouldn't get married again. Not because it was a terrible experience, but I just had no desire to remarry. She accepted this, even if she wasn't happy with it. People have all kinds of luggage and shit with them when they come into a relationship, right? It's up to us to unpack the suitcase and put the stuff where it belongs, but sometimes we don't even realize we are toting luggage and when we do, it can be hard as hell to come to grips to get rid of the junk.

Whether it was, me and my boys and the cheap wine or sometimes just me and the cheap wine at the house, both combinations led to arguments and fights between Debbi and I. Each argument made me want to be without her, but at the same time, I did love her.

Marie...........

Marv called to have a locksmith come make a key for his car. While they were doing that I apologized for him having to spend dough for a locksmith, but I didn't regret what I'd done, he had earned it. I went about my day, it was Saturday, I wasn't doing anything special, just a typical day. Monica and I had left home, we'd gone over to my cousin's place. Meanwhile, Marvin had gotten the key made, then he came got his car and left without saying good-bye to anybody.

When I came home that evening around five thirty, I'd had Leya come by she was at my parent's house waiting for me. We hung out in the yard having drinks while listening to the radio, WBLS.

About ten o'clock everybody had gone in their houses for the night. It was now almost midnight, Monica and I were laying in my bed nodding over the television, when I saw car lights pull up in the driveway. I just didn't feel like getting out of my comfortable spot to be nosey. I heard a knock on my parent's back door, I got up to look out of the window, couldn't fight the curiosity any further. It was Marvin, I went back to my bed and my baby. Then my telephone rang, I knew it was him calling me. I was tempted not to answer the phone, but if I didn't somebody would come out that back door and call out my name, so I picked up the telephone, it was Momma, telling me Marvin's stupid ass adventure. I told her I'd be over there in a minute and hung up the telephone, then I told Monica to stay in the bed, I was going to Grandma's for a few minutes, if she needed anything. I threw on my robe and went to see what was the deal. After I got over there, he started telling my parents and I how he'd gone to the bar right down the highway when he'd left my place this evening, for a drink or two. He's was working on his third Tom Collins when he went to go dance, then he'd come back to the bar to finish his drink, the next thing, he started feeling funny after a few sips of it. So he went to his car, to lie back, you know see if the feeling would go away, if not he'd make it back here. He must have fallen asleep, when he woke up his wallet was gone. Somebody had slipped a micky in his drink and must have watched him go to his car, then followed him out there. His money was gone along with his credit cards, license, everything. He was upset about this, yet at the same time a peek of amusement was in his eyes. He kept a lot of money on

him, he never let you see just how much money he had
on him, you could tell it wasn't just no forty or fifty bucks.
Well over three hundred dollars were in his wallet most of
the time and I took it somebody else had seen this too.
After telling us what had happened, he started making
phone calls to cancel credit cards and all that. I told him
I was sorry for what had happened, he could stay at my
place, and that I had to get back to the house Monica
was home alone sleeping. I went on home and got back
in my bed, Monica had woken up and gotten in her bed
while I was gone. So I went in her room to check on her.
Marv stayed and talked with my folks must have been
another thirty minutes. Then he had the nerve to come
into my bedroom taking off his shirt, like this was his
normal resting place. I didn't say anything to him about it,
he'd had a hard enough weekend. He got in the bed and
put his arm around me, I told him to hold up a minute, so
I could turn the television off. Mean while I came back to
bed and snuggled up to him and we fell asleep. He was
exhausted and probably a bit drowsy from whatever had
been put in his drink.

The next morning we got up things were good,
with still a touch of something just not being right. He left
heading back to Boston to straighten out his cards, license
and changing his locks on his house just to be sure. Pretty
much our relationship stayed on rocky ground, so I knew
I'd play it easy and take it as it came.

People hadn't noticed my alcohol consumption,
back during this time it was normal to have a few drinks
daily and surely expected at social gatherings, and sociable
I was. Friends, cousins, neighbors and I were always
visiting on the regular. Inside I may have kind of still
loved my ex-husband, but had a great dislike for him or a
hate for the things he had done, because of all the shit I'd
gone through with him or because of being in love with

him. He was my first boyfriend, sexually. I guess that made him a little special in my heart. Along with what was a good life growing up it had brought some ugly experiences too, such as my parents fighting like cats and dogs when I was growing up, a family member attempt to persuade me to sleep with him. Whether people know it or not, all things seen or experienced in life shapes you in some shape, form or fashion, even daily wear and tear one goes through day in and day out. Let's see, like you've had a hard day, a drink or puff or something to eat to relax. You can do this more and more frequently to relax and unwind before you know it, it's become a habit. They say, if you do something thirty days in a row it's now become a habit. I wasn't drinking to get a quick drunk on, a drink could last an hour or two. Everything was still running on schedule in our lives. We were well taken care of, clean house, bills paid, my daughter was getting good grades.

I had finished beauty school and had decided I could do better by working from home at this point. So I got a job in the education system so my hours would be the same as Monica's. Then I'd do hair after my day job at school and on Saturdays until about one o'clock in the afternoon. It was easy to make my own schedule.

I was so well liked on my new job at school they talked to me and was offering to help pay for me to go to college to become a teacher. You know I had started out working part time in the cafeteria, then became a teacher's aid. The kids from school loved me, and I enjoyed them greatly. They kept me laughing, kids say and do some of the funniest things, but they usually do them so innocently. Sometimes while we were on summer or holiday break some of the kids would come to visit me at home. I'd make lemonade and snacks for them and they'd hang out with me laughing and talking, telling about their summer adventures and telling grown folks business too.

Most times I kept a man friend handy, like Frankie, he was in the Navy. We had actually grown up together, my second best friends' brother. He always came to see me every little chance he got, called me from around the world. Well, Frankie and I got to diggin' each other more and more, started going steady after a while. Frankie even gave me a beautiful engagement ring, a cluster of diamonds. A few people said, he and I wouldn't get married. Somebody in his family had roots or something on him. Well, as time went on, Frankie started drifting away from me. Calling me less, I couldn't call him as often as I would have liked to, because often he was at sea. As I was saying he was calling less, didn't get to town as often. Then there was the time there was a rumor that Frankie had come to town and hadn't come to see me. Well, I called his sister to ask if Frankie was in town, she answered, "Yes, I thought he had been to your place." I told her to have him call me. He got my message and called about two hours later. I asked him when did he get in, he answered, "I got in late yesterday. I know I didn't tell you I was here, but I had some things to take care of, so I figured I'd do that, then I'd have the rest of my time with you. While listening to him talk I was thinking to myself, this lying motherfucker. I bit my tongue to keep from saying what I really wanted to say and so I said in a calm tone, "Oh baby, that's good. When are we getting together? Tell you what, I'll come pick you up."
He agreed to this suggestion, told me he'd be ready in forty-five minutes.
We hung up the telephone and I went to my bedroom, picked up the telephone to call my Aunt Kate, I had to see if she'd take care of Monica until tomorrow. I knew she would, but I would never just drop Monica off without

asking first. Although Aunt Kate always said yes, she was a pretty lady that always had a man or two chasing her. So with that taken care of, I starting going through my closet trying to find something to wear, nothing too sexy, just a little something to catch his eye. I put on my faux hairpiece and combed the front of my hair to blend in with the hairpiece, then applied my make up. From here I went in my daughter's bedroom grabbed her little over night bag and packed her clothes to spend the night with my aunt. I got everything I needed to take with me, then went to the door and called Monica inside to wash her hands and face. We got in my car and off we went.

I was angry, nervous and excited on my way to see Frankie. I dropped Monica off first, then proceeded down the street to the stop sign, where I had to try to shake off this anxiety I was feeling. I didn't have much time to rid myself of these feelings, because it was only about a four minute ride to meet him.

Allen............
I hadn't seen my son in some time, but I worried and thought about him all the time. I finally asked my mother what did she think about me not seeing him much. She told me, Trina would never bad mouth you and to be patient, when your son is old enough he'll find you. This eased my mind for a short time. A few months past and one day I was in my bedroom and my little sister was standing at the bedroom door we were talking. I asked an eleven or twelve year old what did she think about me missing my son, but staying away from him, me wondering will he remember me, will he want to see me. She told me the same thing my mother had told me. He'll find you when the time comes. I had to give her a hug. We were a close family, but my little sister was special to

us. I guess because she was quite younger than us. Taz and I went downstairs and set on the porch for a while listening to the radio pumping out the latest hits. Then I told Taz to let's go inside for a few. We went in the living room, I picked up my electric guitar and she sat at her drums I had bought for her. She wanted to be a drummer, eventually Pop started dragging her to guitar lessons. I usually bought her musical instruments and even took her to buy her first record when she was five years old. Anyway, we played and made noise to a few records I put on the stereo. After we had finished our performance she went outside to play and I went back to sitting on the porch with the music keeping me company. In case you hadn't figured it out, Debbi had split, she packed up and moved out, she was sharing a place with a girlfriend of hers. She had been gone for three weeks and had only called me once, and ain't this some shit, she didn't give me her number. I probably would have called her, just to check her out, you know just see how she was doing. I did miss her, but knew our relationship was over, it would be selfish to tie up her time, and this ending is what we both needed. I wasn't even thinking of dating right now, just taking time to myself. Taking a break from females, I figured when I was ready I'd date, nothing serious or too consecutive. I didn't want to give some woman the wrong impression that I wanted to move our casual dates to anything more than that.

As I was setting on the porch one of my boys called to see if I wanted to ride with him to south Jersey. I wasn't doing anything and today was Friday, I figured why not. So I told Steve sure I'd be ready. My main man, JoJo had moved to Texas and I did miss him a lot. JoJo and I could read each other's thoughts without saying anything or even looking at each other. I got myself together for Steve to pick me up, shortly he pulled up and blew his car horn. I ran out to his car after locking my place up. We were heading down the highway toward a town about twenty minutes west of Atlantic City. When we arrived it looked like a place that nothing was going on, ever. I had found out on the way there he had some chick he was going out with today, and that she had a friend for me. I was like, "Damn I'm not prepared". Steve was like, relax man, you're fine. Then I started thinking is she going to be unattractive, was she going to get on my nerves or be stupid. I laid back and prepared to just accept what would happen tonight. We got out of his car and walked to her door, the door opened his date was fine. I was hoping to myself - like that saying went, "birds of a feather flock together". My date wasn't in the room, the three of us greeted each other and I was introduced to his date and just as Toni, that was her name, as soon as she told me to have a seat her friend entered the room. I was happy as hell she was fine and had all I liked in the right places. I stood up to greet her, Lynn was smokin' fine. Steve had told me on the way to our dates, I needed something to help get me back on track. Guess what, Lynn had the right things to help me. We went to Atlantic City for dinner and dancing. As far as I could see Atlantic City needed a facelift. It was poor and dangerous looking to me. Just the boardwalk area was nice, but we had a really good time. This chick was fine, friendly and smart and she had turned this brother on. After dancing half the night, we figured we'd better take Toni and Lynn home. As we pulled in front of their place, Toni asked if we wanted to come in. She said they didn't think Steve and I should try to drive home with it being so late and because we had been drinking. To be honest I was tired and Steve was about drunk, he wasn't a sloppy drunk, but I knew how we was. So we all went in, Lynn told me to follow her and gladly I did. She led me to her bedroom and I was damned glad she had led me there too. We sat on the bed and talked for a few minutes, she showed me where the bathroom was and told me to make myself at home. I went to the bathroom and returned back to the bedroom, she had turned on a dimmer light and had gotten in bed already and I joined her after I undressed. As I tried to get settled in her bed moving around my leg touched hers, and she touched my arm, from this point we continued touching and rubbing. This grew to kissing and sucking, from sucking to licking and the next thing you know I was positioned between her beautiful legs pressing up against her, then inside of her, we were starving for each other. We satisfied each other over and over again, the next thing we knew the sun was starting to shine through the bedroom window. That's when we thought, maybe we had better get some sleep. Man, Steve and I ended up spending the whole weekend with these girls. I had a great time, to be honest Lynn and I kept in touch for a short while, somehow we drifted apart. All right, we drifted apart because I put too much space between us. I had taken a drink or two, while I sat back thinking and reflecting on all this. I kept myself unavailable to her emotionally, I didn't really want a relationship right now, but she kind of did. I was ready to enjoy my freedom, even if I did get lonely once in a while. The bed can be a lonely ass place, especially on those nights when it's raining outside or you can here the wind whipping outside your window and you just want to snuggle and cuddle, just have someone to watch television with and eat in bed with. Like most men after it's too late and shit, then I realized maybe I'll call Lynn and try to get with her, not jump right into a relationship but work towards developing one. When I called her she had met somebody else by this time, yep she had a boyfriend now. She told me, "Four months of you not returning my phone calls, now you call me. I stopped calling you, because you never called me, it was always me that was doing the calling. I got tired of chasing you and didn't want to feel as though I was throwing myself at you."

When I was able to squeeze in a word, we did talk for a few minutes after she checked my ass, she had her point, but I didn't lead her to thinking anything would become of us, except an enjoyable casual friendship. See, this is another reason why I was taking it slow with getting back into the dating game, because there is usually drama, drama and more drama. Oh well, back to the drawing board, I'd call her in another few weeks just to say hi again and see if the ole boy was still hanging around. Until then I decided to call another chick to see what was up.

Junie............
    Paula's time had come, we had a baby boy, a cute little thing with big round brown eyes. We were struggling to make it financially, I preferred Paula to stay home to raise our family. Neither of us wanted someone else raising our kids and we'd just be getting the end of the day with our children, or be unhappy because of something they'd been taught by somebody else. We'd gotten everything we needed for our baby, and with the help of family and friends our little boy had more than enough of everything. We had turned the biggest closet in our apartment into his little nursery area. The baby was about ten months old when my parent's asked Paula and I if we wanted to live in the house I had grown up in. My folks had moved, but still had two other houses they rented out. We jumped at the thought of this, we knew everybody in the entire community. To be honest we lived in a nice neighborhood in this apartment complex, but Paula

wasted no time when it came to packing our stuff up to move. The new house had three bedrooms, the yard was large with a fence all around it, this would be great for our dogs, now we wouldn't have to walk them we could just let them out into the yard. It also had a three room work house in the backyard for my lawn equipment and tools. I had learned this trade from working as a little boy with my Grandfather and two of my other little cousins, then I worked with his son, my Uncle C doing lawns. My Uncle C now had a taxi service going and had opened a restaurant. I was actually less then a year old when my grandpa started taking me with him to cut grass. It had taken us about seven weeks to move into the house.

I'm going to tell you, between working days, going to school part time, cutting lawns, and spending time with my family, some days I was so tired it took all I had to make it. Thinking about how long it would be until I finished school, was something I couldn't think about or concentrate on, because that would be enough to make me give up on school. So I just took it one day at a time and prayed for strength and we kept pressing on.

Marie............

Once I arrived in front of Frankie's sister door, I was almost tingling from nerves. I wanted to confront the woman I had grown up with, his sister, about what I had heard some people saying about her having him tied up some kind of way, but what could I say? Come on now, first of all it's something people don't really talk about and when they do talk about it, they're saying is doesn't exist. She saw me pull up and park in front of her door. She opened the door and stepped out, smiling. She was motioning with her hand while telling me to come on in. I was getting out of the car and closing my door as I smiled and headed towards the steps to the house. Lydia held the door open as I entered, steady running her mouth about the usual things. How are you doing, what' cha been up to, and giving me the run down on some of her business. The both of us went into her living room and had a seat, I stood up and walked over to the photos she had hanging on the wall. My back was to Frankie as he entered the room from down the hallway, he seemed happy to see me. I say seemed, because it's pretty easy to put a smile on a face. It would be the hug and kiss that would tell the story. The hug and kiss seemed almost one hundred percent genuine; maybe it was ninety-five percent genuine. Well then, what was the other five per cent? I intended to know the answer to this question before the day was over. He offered to drive, so I held out my hand to give him my keys, but he said he'd drive his car. Your car I said with a question in my voice, he was like, "Yeah, I drove here. Didn't tell you, I'll be for a minute. I'll be here for three weeks. How ya like that?" I was glad and smiling all big in response to him telling me that news. Then he gave me another hug and a real kiss. Well alright I thought, that's more like it. We called to Lydia we'd see her later and we headed for the garage where his Grand Prix was parked. We just road for a while checking out everything and everybody, I had to ask him, "What was up with you?" He was like what are you talking about.

I said, "You know, not hearing from you often and why are you staying at your sister's place when you could be staying at my place? Shit like that."

Frankie answered back, "I was so busy and mentally preoccupied I just didn't pick up the phone, baby. As for me staying at my sister's that's just force of habit, I'm used to staying there I guess because that's where I've always stayed before when I was in town. No thing, I'll be at your place most of the time anyway, right."

I said, "Yes, I hope you're at my place most of the time. Why not bring your stuff to my place, though?"

He replied, "I can see my whole family, if I stay at Lydia's, they stop by, you know."

My response was, "They can stop by where ever you're staying. If you and I are engaged, the next step is marriage, so I'm sure they kind of expect to visit you at my place."

I could see he was going to defend his position with staying at his sister's. While I was thinking this to myself, he added, "Some nights I'll go out with the boys and I'll be coming in late and I don't want to be disrespectful to you and your daughter, also."

Good answer I thought, good answer. "I'm not putting restrictions on you, you'd come and go as you please. I'd just enjoy having you around and knowing we'd share the same bed when you do return. No problem though, stay at your sister's.

Although after not seeing me for months at a time, I figured you might be glad to share my bed with me."

After this little discussion we were quiet for a few minutes, a bit of tension was in the air, but I wasn't going to make a thing out of this. I proceeded on to another conversation to lighten the atmosphere. We hung out popping in some of everywhere that day and ended up at my place around seven thirty. We were tired, yet a bit horny. By the time we fumbled into the living room kissing and tugging at each other's clothes. Child, we didn't even make it to the sofa, we made it to the floor, hot with passion and desire. You know the shit was good, I hadn't had sex in months, since he was last here. I was starving for him to enter me and so he did. Afterwards, he rolled over and looked at me smiling, telling me that I was a beast and how he enjoyed it. After we had gotten the strength to get up off the floor we made it to the sofa. We had picked up some cooked seafood dinners while we were on our way to my place. So we started nibbling, no not on each other, on the food this time, but before we finished our plate, the plates were set aside, as he started touching my breasts and rubbing my thigh. How did I respond to his touch, I opened my legs a bit more so he could rub the inside of my long thighs, umh, this was nice, I thought as I relaxed to his caress. I wished we could be together like this anytime we wanted. This Navy thing was getting in the way, but that was a career choice he'd made and wanted to see it through. After we'd made love again, we had fallen asleep on the sofa for a while, when Frankie awoke I had been up for some time. He asked, "Do you think you and I are going to be alright.

I answered, "I sure hope we'll be fine."

He said he believed so too, and asked me to be patient with him, he'd make it worth my while. I smiled at him, but wondered what brought this thought or question to his mind. Then I thought, maybe it's best that I didn't know why he'd brought this up. Maybe he knew something I didn't know?

The telephone rang, it was Frankie's brother Jake, he thought he was so damned cool, and he was pretty cool and smooth I had to give it to him. He wasn't fine or anything like that, but women seemed to go for him, because he was style was smooth and cool. His brother and I were buddies also he wanted to know what we were doing and he invited us to his place for a card game and cookout. "Not a lot of folks, just the usual group, "he said.

I told him, "Hold on, I'll let you speak to your brother."

I handed to phone to Frankie, he was always down for a card game. It would have been nice to stay home and enjoy some time to ourselves, now we'd be gone most of the night, but we'd have a good time. These card games consisted of drinking, dancing, smoking, cards and a whole lot of bullshit talking. I didn't play cards too much, but I was down with the rest of the fun. So we started getting ourselves together to head on to his brother's place or as Jake's. Frankie played cards a whole lot in the military, he could cheat like hell and people wouldn't even know what was going on. He could stack the deck and do all kinds of card tricks and so could Jake. So it was about to be a bunch of trash talking, cussing and laughs.

We stopped by the liquor store to get some vodka, scotch, mixers and ice. When we arrived at Jake's the crew was there pretty much. We went inside his apartment, the grill was outside in the grass by the front door, some people were setting on the steps and the rest were inside. After I spoke to everybody, I walked down to my Aunt Kate's she lived the next building over, Monica was at my Aunt's for the night, Leya and Dave walked with me. We visited them for about half an hour, Aunt Kate and Monica were waiting for my Mom and sister to pick them up, they were riding down to the beach. So we went back to the get together. They had already started talking shit about everything under the sun. Yes, the lying competition had begun. I was walking in the door with one of the world's best bullshitters, my cousin Dave. Dave was in the Army, but he was here from North Carolina. He and Frankie told stories about their military experiences being away from home, and they had us cracking up. Leya just had straight up funny stories, but it was the way she talked, seriously, she was the female Richard Pryor. She cursed every few words, but it was funny for real. I told them about when my cousin's from Baltimore had came up last time and I had gotten so tore up, it was raining big ass cats and dogs and I went home in a taxi barefoot. I didn't even know my shoes were missed until the next day when I was looking for my sandals and Mo told me I came home barefoot. So I had called my Mama and she was like, yes your shoes are in the den. She and I fell out cracking up at this episode.

Frankie and Jake was beating the snot out everybody they played, then Dave said, "These mothers are cheating as usual."
That's all it took Frankie started trying to convince people he wasn't cheating, voices had gotten loud. So Frankie always being the calm one of the bunch, was like, "Never mind, let's just forget the game, I didn't cheat every hand. That's how ya'll got some points, so ya'll should be grateful to me."

After the game ended he and I headed back to my place. I was tipsy and he was almost drunk, it was all we could do to get in the bed, believe me, nothing went on after getting in the bed, nothing but sleep.

It was about ten o'clock Sunday morning when the phone rang, it was his sister. "Hi Marie, can I speak to Frankie for a minute, "she said.
"Hold on", was all I said to her, because I knew this wasn't a good thing that she had called. She had some small drama she needed him to help her with. He told her he'd be there in about two hours. About and hour later the telephone rang again, it was her once more.
"I'm sorry to be a bother, but can I speak with Frankie again."
I had to ask her, "Is something wrong?"
"Of course, if it wasn't I wouldn't bother the two of you", she responded.
All I could do was sigh as I called him out the bathroom to the telephone again. He knew this shit she was doing was bogus, but he would always jump when she called for him.

Then I remembered my car was at his sister's. I said to him, "Give me ten minutes to get myself ready. My car is at your sister's."

I got in his car with him, we chatted some, while there was a slight tension in my chest because, I wanted to lay her ass out and him too, for jumping like a motherfuckin' puppet.

He and I kissed as I got in my car, then I went to get my daughter, neither she or my Aunt were there, so I came on home and there they were just walking in my parent's back door. I went inside behind them so we could have girl talk. My Papa was at the kitchen table so he joined in the girl talk a little. Papa always told me the real deal about men, he used to be a real player and he could read in between the lines and clarify things to me. Now whether I listened to him or not that was a different story. Most times I took pointers from him, because he was usually right.

As I was leaving, walking out the door I was thinking about calling Lydia to talk to her about always interfering with me and Frankie, it wasn't like I saw him all the damn time, when I saw my brother Allen walking towards the door. He had a look on his face like he was thinking about something, but it was a good thought, because he had a smile on his face before he'd even seen me. Allen and I hugged and exchanged a few words in the driveway before he went inside and I went home.

I hung around my place waiting to see if I'd hear from Frankie again today, but I wasn't going to be surprised if I didn't see him again today, it wouldn't be the first time. Monica had come home while I was at my parents' talkin, she was in her bed watching television. A few hours later, I'd say about seven forty-five in the evening when my telephone rang. I'd been a sipping a drink or two, while hanging around the house. I answered the phone, it was him saying he was going to try to get back over to my place. His sister had gone out about three hours ago and asked him to keep an eye on her son, she'd be back in about two hours. I said okay, just let me know if you're going to make it or not. Eighty thirty I put my night gown on and got in my bed with a cocktail on my night table, and I found a good old movie to settle down with, I didn't hear from the bastard anymore that night. I started to go to his sister's, but instead I called my girl, Leya. We talked about the shit that was going on, she told me she was going to go by to see if Fankie was there. She was leaving as soon as we hung up the phone and she'd call me back or come by my place. We hung up, thirty minutes later, I heard a knock at my door, I went to peep out, just to make sure who was there, it was Leya. She had just rode by to see what she saw. Leya said, "His car is there and so is hers. So why hasn't the nigga called you back. See that's why you have to fuck them up, it keeps his shit on point. If you want me to I'll go knock on the door to see what the fuck is happenin'. Don't let him or his motherfuckin' sister play you."

I thought about what she was saying, should I go over there? I called my mother to tell her I was bringing Monica over there for about an hour and a half, Momma said the back door is open. I got my baby out her bed and dropped her off. Leya and I got in her Volkswagon and off we went to check this out thoroughly. We pulled up to Lydia's house, I went to ring the doorbell, she answered the door. "Hi, I need to speak with Frankie", I said as I entered the house before she could invite me in. She was telling me she was sorry for the inconvenience, she had gotten back a little while ago and Frankie was asleep. Were ya'll supposed to get together?

"No not really," I told her, "could you get him for me?"

"Come on, he's back here," she said as we walked down the hallway.

Lydia asked me if anybody was waiting for me, she knew that was Leya's car, I said "Yes, Leya's out there."

I tapped on the bedroom door where he was sleeping. He answered come in, he seemed surprised to see me as I entered the room. I sat on the side of the bed and I asked him what the hell was up? No beating around the bush or being nice about it. Tell me what's going down? He started telling me about his day and all that happened to hold him up from coming back over. Hell, I could have come over here with Monica. It's not like all of us are strangers, your family and mine grew up together, Monica and Sam play together on a regular. He said I thought she'd be back shortly, because of what she had told me.

I said to him, "I don't know but, it seems she enjoys keeping your dumb ass busy, or distracted?"

We went back and forth and voices got louder, then he got up out the bed saying he didn't feel like hearing all this. I was like you don't feel like hearing the truth then? "Whatever the fuck it is, I don't want to hear it now. I was sleep and you woke me up fussing," he was yelling.

I had to stand up to respond, "You don't have to hear a damned thing, because I'm tired of this dumb shit. I see you every couple of months and when you're here you're always stuck up in this house. Well you keep on staying stuck up in here, don't bother to call me anymore. I mean it, don't call me no damned more," I told him. I really did mean this.

I walked out the bedroom door and down the hall back to the door to the front porch. Leya was standing outside her car, smoking, she said she was standing out the car in case she had to run in there and kick somebody's ass. His sister had tried to come between Leya and Jake, but Jake didn't let it happen. Just then Frankie came out the door, telling me to bring my ass back there. I kept right on going.

"Get back here, Marie. I mean it. If I come down there," he was saying.

"If you come down here, you'll get your ass kicked if you touch me. Take care," I called to him as Leya and I got in her car. She started the engine and we drove back home. I wanted to be quiet on the way home, but I needed to vent, I had to vent some to Leya, I thanked her for her help, as I got out of her car and then went inside my place. I was feeling mad, hurt, disappointed and tired of men fucking things up. Then they want to try to fix the messed up relationship, afterwards.

All I could do was take a deep breath and sigh a few times as I got ready for bed. Really though, I was finished being patient with him, because things weren't getting better, he was allowing nothings to get between the two of us. If that's the way he wanted it, then so be it. It takes two to make a relationship work.

I'd gotten to sleep then having to go to the bathroom interrupted my sleep so I went to the bathroom and had just gotten back in bed, when the telephone rang. I knew who it had to be, unless it was a wrong number. I answered it, it was Frankie trying to smooth things, but I told him in a calm voice, that I meant the things I had said. Let's just leave things alone between us, and go our separate ways. I offered to give him the engagement ring back, he seemed to think it over for a second or two, then said, no for me to keep it. I responded with, "Okay, then take care. I was just about to go back to sleep." I wanted to cry, but wasn't quite sure why I wanted to cry, maybe because it was another chapter ending or closing. I hung up the phone, but couldn't get to sleep for a while. He called me again the next morning to tell me he was on his way over. Even after he arrived, we sat in the living room and discussed the things that had happened and why I was ready to call it quits. He agreed I had a good point and that it was a good idea to take a break. Then he gave me a hug before he walked back to his car. Was it that he wanted something to break us up or was he just wrapped up and didn't know any better. Nope, he wasn't naive a bit, he wanted out and this was his way.

Allen.............

I had gone out with Lynn, just a friendship thing, you know, we'd had a good time. She came to see me and we spent most of the day together, of course she didn't spend the night, I didn't even try her. I was a gentleman, sometimes that seemed to make women curious. She's a nice girl, but she has that boyfriend. I was willing to accept this now, and just go with the flow, plus I had a few other females I spent time with.

My brother had wanted to talk to me about something, so I was going to meet my brother here at my parent's today for a talk.

Junie..............

I spent a lot of time with my wife and baby. As I got my son ready to ride with me to meet my brother, Paula laid on the sofa. She looked tired today, like she needed a break. I told her to pamper herself, take a relaxing shower or bath, put on something comfortable, light some candles and kick back. We'd be back later so she could have the afternoon to herself. Our relationship usually ran pretty smooth, don't get me wrong we had our ups and downs, but we were very compatible.

I stopped by my Uncle C's for a few before I went to meet my brother. I had to show the family how the baby was growing. I made it to my parents' house, me and my brother nibbled on food we found in the fridge, then we went on the porch to talk. Not really talk about just one topic, although I did mention him drinking too much. He didn't want to hear it, he told me he liked drinking and could stop if he wanted to, but he didn't want to. I told him sometimes when he drank he did things that didn't make any sense and to be careful, then we talked about his female friends and I talked about my more than busy schedule. We both loved sports, so we had to update each other on the latest headlines. I then went inside to ask if they'd watch the baby while me and Allen went for a short ride. We just cruised for a while, you know we needed some brotherly time. It felt good to have some down time and relax with him, we hadn't done this in a long time. We kept it real with each other.

When we got back to the house, I stayed for a few minutes, but I was too tired to stay a long time. I had already dosed off while watching television with my dad, so I got my son and headed for home to get in the bed by seven o'clock.

Paula had dinner ready, although I had told her not to do anything, to just rest. I got my plate of food, ate and went right to bed. I had to get up early tomorrow to start a long day. She understood me not wanting to set around and talk or anything else. Paula had on a sensuous smelling perfume, she smelled like she wanted something. You know what she wanted. She didn't call me big daddy for nothing. I got in the bed, she came in the room and massaged my back until I fell asleep. I had been sleeping for about an hour, then I woke up and started kissing Paula on the back of her shoulder, this sent a tingle to her meaty butt cheeks. She turned over to face me almost immediately. She had a shapely and full figured built, I grabbed a hand full of hip and it was on from there.

Allen...............

I had been drinking this day, I had decided I was going to see Deb this day. I called and told the police I'd be coming through their town. It was a town where the police were known for pulling people over for the slightest of anything. I got in my car and went flying up the highway, I was doing about seventy in a forty-five mph zone. The police would have stopped me even if I hadn't called to let them I was coming. As I was flying up the highway in that darn town, they gave me a speeding ticket and said I couldn't drive home, I'd have to have someone come get me and my car. I called my man Steve to come get me, he had a girlfriend come with him to the police station to pick me up. Steve drove me home to my parents. Mom was sitting on her front porch when we pulled up, after I got out the car I told my mother what had happened. She wasn't happy about my actions and that was putting it mildly. I went inside to lay on my parent's couch. After I sobered up, I went into the kitchen where my mother was peeling potatoes. My Pop was upstairs changing clothes. My mother told me to take a piece of raw potato, it would take the liquor smell off my breath, my little sister was looking at me eat the potato, like "Ilk." Her face was all torn up with distaste. Mom then told me she'd take me home and for me to straighten myself up, but first she told me I acted like a fool, calling the police on myself. I agreed with her, how in the world could I not agree. Mommy told me to go on before my father came back downstairs and there be some trouble. Pop would eventually hear about this I'd hear it from him another time, but I thought it would be better to hear it later. Man, I wasn't happy with how I had fucked up. I got a speeding ticket, drunken driving ticket, and would have to go to some classes to help get points off my license after this stunt. My mom and I walked to her car for her to take me home. By the time I reached my place, I had decided I needed a break from drinking. I had been doing stupid shit, getting myself in trouble, not big trouble, but it could lead up to real trouble. I mean after I sobered up I'd regret acting a fool. Anyway, I made it inside my crib, took off my clothes and got right in the shower, I was still a bit tipsy. I heated some leftovers, and sat on my bed in my drawers watching television waiting for my food to get warm. I found me a good movie, got my food and a huge glass of iced tea. I lived a block from the ocean, there was always a lovely breeze blowing through my windows, usually I didn't even need a fan. With the ocean breeze blowing through my windows, sometime before midnight I fell asleep.

The next morning I woke up to a beautiful sunny day. I walked out into my yard to see the sun still coming up over the ocean. The air was fresh and cool. I walked to the beach to a telephone and called my job to let them know I wouldn't be in today. Instead of going to work, I took care of my business, paid bills and dropped in to see my Uncle J for a minute. I got to my Uncle J's crib about noon, he was setting on his porch that was fully decorated with artificial flowers, a television and a fan. He was eating his lunch and told me to join him, and so I did.

He didn't try to be like, he was like Sammy Davis Jr. His family was doing fine, so I left there and went to grocery shopping. The store I stopped in wasn't my usual, I usual went over by my parents to shop. Over near my parents they had new well kept stores, they were the first to have the storm effects on the vegetables and fruits to keep them fresh. This day I stopped in another neighborhood, it wasn't a bad neighborhood, but the store tended to cater to the poorer folks. I got a few items to hold me over until next weekend when I'd do my real shopping. While I was in line waiting to pay for my food, the female employee at my register was been bickering with the lady working at customer service. They got to yelling to each other, then the woman at the register where I was yelled clean across the store, calling the other woman a bitch. I was like, I be damned. They were raising so much hell with each other and the manager was trying to handle the situation between his employees and attempting to calm his customers. I started to leave my basket of food and just go to the store I normally shopped at, but I didn't feel like driving all the way to the other store, shopping again, then driving back home. So I bared the ignorance that was going on, paid for my stuff and made it home to my little sanctuary with it's relaxing breeze.

I still hadn't seen or talked to Deb since I had called to tell her I was coming to see her. So I decided to call her right then from the telephone at the store, I picked up the receiver, then second thought not to call her. I hung the phone up, put my food in the car and went home. I was relaxing eating my chocolate chip cookies, when I heard a light tap at my door, I could see her face in the screen. It was Deb, I opened the door and invited her inside. She told me she had someone waiting for her, just a minute she'd be right back, she was going to tell her friend she could leave. As she walked to the car to talk to her friend, I was looking at Debbi, she had put on a few pounds, she looked good. I hadn't seen her a few months. She came back inside, I fixed her a glass of ice cold Pepsi, that was her drink. She seemed a bit nervous, but I guess I was too. Then I asked her if she wanted anything to eat, she didn't want anything. We talked and watched television for a few hours, then she decided it was time for her to go home. We didn't bring up trying to get back together, just updated each other on what was going on in our lives. After we had finished talking I offered to take her home, of course she accepted. I put a shirt on and my shoes, got my keys and off we went. We drove along the beach for a few miles headed in the direction of her place. As I pulled up in front of her apartment, I was hoping she'd invite me in. She kissed me on my cheek and said she'd talk to me later. I guess it was good she didn't invite me in, that could have been opening up a can of worms. I drove back home reminiscing about Deb and I and also thinking about Lynn. It was still early when I got back home, so I could mentally relax and get ready for work the next day.

I went about my regular daily schedule for the next few weeks, except no drinking. I did spend one Saturday night with Lynn, she came up to see me. I asked her what would your boyfriend think about this. She smiled and said, "He probably wouldn't even care. That's if he even noticed she wasn't home. I don't see him much at all. To be honest, I believe he's seeing someone else. I'm waiting for him to tell me, before I have to tell him about him seeing somebody other than me. I know he's seeing another woman. So I'm not worried about it and neither should you."

We enjoyed a nice weekend, she was a sweet girl, and fine. Why was I dragging my feet, just not willing to get into a relationship that probably would have been so good for me. A fool, that's what Steve had said I was. I'd probably mess around and let her slip away then regret it. Who knows, maybe I'd get rid of these cold feet of mine before it was too late.

Marie............

As for me I was taking a break from men, not even going on a date. Uhm, men, who wants em? Who needs em? They're nothing but turmoil and drama. Straight up trouble, that's what they are.

Work, family and friends were enough for me. Not saying I didn't enjoy looking at a fine man, but that was enough for now. No giving my number or taking a telephone number.

It had been close to two years before I started dating again. I decided I was ready for the dating scene again, did I miss the ups and downs they brought with them or was I an optimist, thinking just maybe, there's one out there right for me.

Anyway, I started dating, but taking it slow. Once I went on a date I didn't even call him until a week later. Didn't let them come to my house unless my daughter wasn't home. I didn't want her to meet anybody I wasn't serious about.

Life was fine, nothing exceptional going on. This weekend coming up Monica and I were going to south Jersey to visit Sherrie. Remember her, she was my sister-in-law. We always kept in touch and visited each other regularly. I was taking the bus down, this bus ride by car took an hour and a half ride, the bus turned it into an all day event. My daughter hated taking the bus, but I didn't drive out the area we lived in. So early Saturday morning we got up got dressed and I got Monica's little snack bag that we shared on our ride to see Sherrie. My mom and little sister drove us to the bus station, our bus left at eight-thirty in the morning., we arrived at one-thirty that afternoon. This bus stopped for every thing and wiggled its' way through almost every town and back dirt road, by car this would have been an hour and half ride.

Monica had cousins here to play with, while Sherrie and I sipped on cocktails with her sister and laughed our asses off. Sherrie's sister was married with four children, we stayed around her place so she didn't have to bother to get somebody to take care of the kids. Later that evening Monica stayed with Sherrie's sister, while Sherrie and I went out that night. We didn't stay out too late, because I was tired from the ride and drinking cocktails during the afternoon.

We'd had a nice time and headed back to pick up Monica in the middle of the night. I didn't want to wake her up, but we were staying at Sherrie's, that was on the other side of town and I knew I didn't want to get up early to have to go get her. Sunday we slept late, when we woke up Sherrie had already cooked a delicious breakfast. I adored breakfast food, even if it didn't keep my stomach full.

We sat at the kitchen table and talked about the people that lived on our street when Sherrie and her husband moved down the street from my family. How the world seemed so sunny, bright and happy then and how times and things had changed, including us. Some of the ole' gang had moved out of state, we didn't keep in close contact but when they were in town how we'd all get together and it was like we been seeing each other all along. Sherrie was still head over heels in love with her ex-husband and didn't care who knew it. She told everybody how she still had such love and desire for that man. He'd had a woman that was willing to do anything for him, but instead he liked the streets and chasing other women. She had even thought the reason why he finally left her was because she couldn't have a baby, she did have some medical reason for having a difficult time conceiving. Her doctor wanted her husband to come in for a sperm count and he wouldn't go. So she kept asking him, after months her husband agreed to go have the sperm count done, come to find out his sperm count was low. Maybe it was low because he had so many women he was fucking. Anyway, about two years past after they finally got divorced, Sherrie got pregnant. She had waited around six years before she divorced him, she was waiting to see if they'd get back together. The chick gave up on it and decided to move ahead with her life. We didn't know who the father was, but for some reason people thought it was her ex-husband's. Sherrie's little girl was adorable she looked quite a bit like her mom.

Let me get back to the story at hand. That Sunday afternoon Monica and I got back on the bus to head for home, we'd had a nice weekend. My ex-husband lived not too far from Sherrie, but Monica didn't see him this visit. I must admit, if he'd known we were in the area he'd have come to get her. He spent as much time as he could with her, she looked so much like her Dad. It was cute to see them together, even if he did get on my nerves.

After our long ride back home, I couldn't wait to get in my place to relax. Monica didn't feel too well, the fumes from the bus had gotten to her. After we settled in and got a bite to eat, she felt better, but I'd have to stop the bus trips, I didn't want my baby sick or poisoned from exhaust. I fixed myself a screwdriver cocktail and phoned Mama. Shortly after I'd hung up from talking with my mother, the telephone rang, it was the guy that I'd gone out with. We had gone on a few dates, he wanted to see me again. Monica was going to bed early tonight, tomorrow was a school day, I got bold and told him to come over around nine o'clock tonight. This way she'd be asleep and wouldn't see him. Like I'd said I didn't want her to meet somebody I didn't think would be a round for a while. He was nice enough, but not want I wanted a real relationship with him. Nine o'clock came and he hadn't shown up, he was twenty minutes late, that was okay. He came in and I fixed him a drink and we sat on the sofa. He was so funny, not like telling jokes funny, just naturally funny. He had me cracking up, I tried to be quieter because I thought I was going to wake Monica up. I suggested that we go to my bedroom to watch television maybe he would be able to make me laugh my clothes off again. Know what I mean? I didn't allow him to stay all night, because I didn't want to chance Monica running into him.

Allen............

I wasn't able to get rid of my cold feet to get with Lynn in a steady relationship, so I missed that boat. I was off from work tomorrow and thought I'd have a few drinks, I had my stereo blasting and the neighbors didn't appreciate this. So after a complaint I turned my music off and turned on the television. For some reason I wasn't able to make myself settle down tonight, I was full of energy, so I decided to go to a bar to socialize. Under the influence, but not drunk I headed for a bar I visited kind of often. The evening was a bit early, people were just getting off from work. The jukebox was pumping, I sat at the end of the bar and talked to the bartender for a few minutes, I'd known him for years. We were talking and shooting the breeze when this dude walked in and took a seat four barstools away from us. He looked familiar to the both of us, yet we couldn't place his face. The dude glanced at us, nothing out of the ordinary, just a glance. The guy stood up and proceeded in our direction at the end of the bar. He was dressed a little sharp and a bit over the edge. He then sat on a barstool one seat away from

where I was setting. The bartender walked over to him
and asked what he could get for them. The guy ordered
a drink when the drink was placed in front of him, he
asked the bartender, "So how are you?" He asked like he
knew the guy behind the bar, "I've been pretty good",
the bartender answered, then excused himself for a few
minutes. Then the dude turned to me and asked what had
I been up to. I said, "A little of everything and some of
nothing. How about you, what you been up to?"

So he started talking and telling about some things he'd
been up out in California. By now I had an idea of who
this guy might be, I interrupted him and asked point
blank, "What's your name?"

By now the bartender had come back over in front of us,
he was trying to figure out this guy's face just like I was.

He answered, "Now come on man, what do you think my
name is?"

I guess I was looking at him in a peculiar way. "Why you
looking at me like that," he asked me.

I said I know a guy named Carl that moved to California
about ten years ago.

The guy said, "Ain't that something. What part did he
move to?"

I told him, "Up near Long Beach."

"I'm from that area, I might even be that same Carl," he
said.

Both the bartender and myself said, "Carl Shanks?"

"It's me in the flesh, baby," the dude said.

We started laughing and hugging. He looked so different,
his eyes looked familiar, but he now had a huge afro and
a thick beard and mustache, pierced ear, and looked older
then his actual age. We all were like I'll be damned. Man,
we drank and talked for hours catching up on life. Carl
used to hang out with my brother pretty often back in
the day. I told him where Junie lived and to look him up,

and I updated him on everybody. By the time we left the bar we were both pretty loaded. I stopped by my parents' house and told them who I had seen. Carl had said to tell them he'd see them tomorrow. I ended up staying at my folks' for a while talking, getting on their nerves, and watching television, before I went on home.

The next day Carl kept his word, he went to see Junie and my parents. They were surprised at how he had changed also, he didn't look bad, just so different. Maybe a little older than the rest of the guys he used to hang out with.

My partner JoJo had called me last week to tell me he'd be in town in two weeks. Man, I couldn't wait to see him. I could think of something and he knew what I was thinking without me opening my mouth and I could do the same with him. JoJo was always going to college, he'd get one degree and before you could turn your head he was back in school for another degree. I told him he's a professional student, been in school twenty-two years, no joke.

Once I got in my door it crossed my mind that I had to work tomorrow, but would like to call out, but I knew I had to show up.

Meanwhile, Lynn was coming over in about two hours and I really needed to freshen myself up. I wanted to see her, but didn't feel like cleaning up, but I straightened up a bit. I also didn't want her to be able to tell I was maybe a little tipsy, you know? I straightened my apartment and had just stepped out the shower and started putting lotion on my feet, when the doorbell rang. It couldn't be her already. I had a towel around my waist as I peaked out the door to make sure I had really heard the doorbell. It rang again, so I put on my robe and went to the door, she was half an hour early. I opened the door and told her to come in. As she entered she gave me a peck on the lips, then went to stand by the kitchen counter, she was holding a paper bag. So I asked what was in the bag, she answered I brought some wine to go with dinner. The last thing I needed was some more alcohol, I didn't even want to smell liquor, but I didn't want to hurt her feelings, so I told her to put it in the fridge and make herself comfortable, while I finished getting myself together. Earlier this morning I had seasoned the food I was cooking for dinner, but now that she had arrived before I was ready, I decided to order Chinese food instead. After I was dressed and smelling good, I came back out to give her a better greeting. I asked Lynn what did she feel like doing, she wanted to go set on the boardwalk, but I suggested we order our food and eat first then stroll to the beach. So we ordered, fried rice with shrimp, shrimp and broccoli, and shrimp toast. While waiting for the food to be delivered we sipped on iced tea, I never let my refrigerator run out a supply of iced tea. I didn't know about her, but I was starving and was thinking about meeting the delivery guy half way to get this grub. I paid for the food and placed it on the table, then pulled out a seat for her, then proceeded to get wineglasses and the wine, as I walked to the table I saw she was fixing our plates. That a girl I thought, she didn't need somebody to do it all for her, she was willing to pitch in. We had a great meal eating, talking and laughing so hard that once some of her fried rice flew out of her mouth. She was fun, I had to give her that, and fine. After we let our food digest for about fifteen minutes I got my keys and said, "Let's go."

There were a lot of people at the beach, we strolled along the boardwalk for a while, looking for a bench to sit on. Every other bench faced the ocean, the benches in between faced the street. We wanted one facing the ocean. After walking what seemed like ten miles, we

got a bench facing the ocean, the breeze was feeling so soothing. She kind of snuggled up next to me. If I had been thinking I would have brought a blanket with us, so we could have laid on the sand. The sun started to set about an hour after we got to the beach we had seen some sights and gotten our laugh on. To be honest, I was kind of ready to go home, but she suggested we stick our feet in the water. Of course, I obliged the lady. I enjoyed the water, and had gotten wet up to my thighs, those waves started feeling good and I had to walk out into the water a bit further. I hadn't been in the ocean in years. When we finally got out of the water, we had to chuckle at each other, because we were like kids in the water. I took her hand at the edge of the water and led her back up onto the boardwalk to head home. As I opened the door she touched my back and slid her hand down to my behind, I remained cool until we got in that door. Then I was all over her, we were ripping off wet clothes, hers weren't just wet from ocean water either. You know what I mean? Right on the floor by the door we went at it, like hungry animals. Naturally we are animals and should let go and act like what we are some times. She laid it on me, afterwards my legs were feeling shaking as we made it to my bed, I was a gentleman and let her rest for a while before I woke her up to get some more of that good stuff. I had to be to work in the morning, so I couldn't be as greedy as I felt like being and make love most of the night. Lynn woke up around three in the morning, I glanced at her as she got dressed. I sat up in the bed, "You leaving now", I asked her.
She answered, "Yes, I have a long ride ahead of me. I'll get home in time to make it to work, if I leave now. You stay in the bed and I'll see my way out. I'll call you when I get home."

I did want to stay in the bed, but I got up and threw on a pair of shorts and walked her to her car, being careful not to wake myself all the way up. Six-thirty, time to get up would be here in shortly, so I got back to sleep right away. Six-thirty nine the phone rang, it was Lynn she was home. We didn't get into a conversation, because I had to be out the door in half an hour. I dragged my ass to work and I'm telling you it was a long workday. I hadn't wanted to come to work in the first place, then being up late last night, everything seemed to be moving in slow motion today.

Thursday came and my supervisor had gotten on my nerves. He tried to write me up on some bull crap. I wasn't having it, because I knew I hadn't done anything wrong. The more I defended my actions the madder it made that bastard. If he was going to write me up, then I was writing him up. On my lunch break, I got me a notepad and pen to begin writing, I was in deep concentration, so I wouldn't leave out any important details of what had happened today or the previous other time he had got on my back. I guess my supervisor figured I was serious about writing him up and came to the table I was setting at to talk to me. He said, he'd had a rough morning and didn't mean to take it out on me. \ I accepted his apology and when he left I continued writing, because I had a feeling this wasn't going to be the last time he'd be acting like an ass. My motto is, hope for the best, but prepare for the worst.

Several days past, here we are at the end of the workweek, thank God. So I'm feeling lighthearted and happy, because first of all I can sleep late tomorrow morning. I'd just finished filing the logs of medications given to patients by the nurses. I was just about to take my morning break, when this crazy ass supervisor came and asked me in a nasty manner to mop the floor in the break area. First that wasn't a part of my job description, secondly he asked me in the wrong way. So I told him I was getting ready to take my break, but also wanted to know why maintenance couldn't get the floor. He said to me, I asked you to mop the floor, not maintenance. I said to him, "No I can not mop the floor. We have maintenance people right here on this floor at our need. Just buzz for one of them. Usually there's someone close by." Then I added, "I don't appreciate the tone of voice you used, either."

It wasn't just me that had run-ins with this asshole, there were five other people complaining about him to our manager, although nothing much seemed to be being done about this idiot. He didn't say anything else about mopping no damned floor, he went about his business and I took my break. Believe me I made a note of this conversation for future reference. You know how you know something else will come up, I knew there was more to come from this ass.

I survived through the rest of the day, being pleasant and looking forward to three thirty, quitting time. A few guys and I from work were going to stop by happy hour after work. I didn't have any plans for afterwards, except to relax and put my feet up. After punched out on the time clock, we all got in our cars and headed to happy hour. Getting off at three thirty is earlier than most other folks, so we got first dibs on the free food they had put out at the bar. I fixed me a little plate and sat at the bar to order my drink. We were shooting the breeze and laughing. I hadn't been to happy hour in a while. Heck this was only my third time coming with the guys. We got to talking about our supervisor and how this dude was trying to see how much he could get away with, talking to people any kind of way. Anybody that knew me, knew I didn't play that. Don't just talk to me any old kind of way, I'd let a person know, back it up and try it again the right way. After close to three hours here I figured I should go by my parents' place for a while. So I headed on over that way. They were all doing fine, my little sister had just walked in the door from playing basketball. She liked the game, but I think she first got into it because my brother and myself played. I remember I had my football uniform under the bed when I was in high school, we didn't have practice that day, when I came home I knew it had been tampered with, it was Taz. She was playing with the uniform. I knew somewhere in the future she'd take to liking football too. Anyway, I didn't stay long, basically just passing through on my way home. I couldn't wait to get a shower and lay out across my bed watching the game tonight with a nice cold beer and some pickled pigs feet. Oh man, that was going to be on the money for me tonight. Next week JoJo would be here, yesterday I had put in my request for three days off. He was coming in on Friday, I figured I'd work that day and take off the following Monday, Tuesday, and the following Friday, I was really looking forward to seeing him.

I had been thinking about my son and wanted to see him, but wasn't sure if I should. I don't know why I hesitated at this. For some reason, I felt it was better to let him be without me. If anything were wrong I'd hear about it from his mom. As I laid across the bed it was eating at me, so I picked up the telephone and called little man to hear his voice. He was doing fine, and he was so happy to talk to me. After hearing his little voice I was able to relax. He didn't sound like a little baby anymore, I was just getting tiny little pieces of his life every now and then, but missing the whole act of him growing up. One thing I did know I wanted him to get an education, and didn't mean just a high school education, nobody in our family, had gone to college. An education would make his life so much easier. I started dozing off at this point, I couldn't tell you what was on the screen, next thing I knew it was two twenty-six in the morning, when I woke up just enough to turn the TV off and roll over for part two. Some time during the night that supervisor ran across my mind, something telling me to be alert.

I awoke all refreshed the next morning figured I'd go do my laundry, while I was there washing clothes I thought to myself I need to play some basketball, my brother's active even with his hectic schedule and bad knee. He walks, plays ball, and swims. It was on, I'd be on the court this afternoon.

Marie.............

If my ex-husband would get his act together and stop chasing women, I'd get back with him, I was thinking this day. I think I would. At one point I enjoyed dating, but this shit was getting tired. By the end of the day, I was back to my ole self, thinking I might never remarry and I pretty much did enjoy my life. Not having to cater to a husband. It's easier taking care of and catering to a child than a grown ass man.

I had gone out with that guy for a few months, nothing on a regular. Just getting together every now and then, kept it casual. I was still taking dating slow. I was working on learning how to drive now, so I could get my license and a car. My cousin Dee and I were the last to get driver's license of any of our cousins or friends our age I had put away a few dollars to buy a little car to get around in. I really figured it was time to drive, it would make life easier, that was for sure.

Junie.................

My knee had been giving me some trouble lately. When I was in high school playing basketball, I took a fall during a game and it tore my knee to pieces. The doctors had said I'd walk with a severe limp or have to use a cane. I couldn't even picture me at the age of seventeen being handicapped, not as much as I loved being athletic and physical. I had reconstructive surgery to rebuild my knee and they put lots of pins and screws in my knee to put it back together hoping it would mend together. It did, but a few of the pins had to remain in my knee, but guess what. I never used no cane or walked with a severe limp. Lately it felt like sometimes my pant legs would get snagged on my knee, I was really feeling some discomfort in my knee, so I went to the doctor to have it checked out. The doctor saw where a piece of metal was working it's way out of my knee through my flesh. I was looking at this guy touching this metal sticking out of my knee, then he got a big pair of tweezers and alcohol pads. I was thinking is he going to pull this out, and if he does is my knee going to come apart somewhere inside. I tried to just let him do his thing, but I had to stop him and ask, "What's going to happen to my knee if you pull that pin out?" The doc said it should be fine. It's been years since your surgery, it must have healed and is pushing the metal out. He pulled the pin out of my knee, and told me if it continued to give me trouble to come back. Then he said, "While you're here I'm going to do an x-ray to see all that's going on inside there." The x-ray showed a few more pins had came loose from the bones. He suggested we wait to see if they'd work their way to the surface and if so he'd them. About nine weeks later another pin came poking out of my knee, there were two other pieces that was giving me trouble though. When I returned to the doctor, his office scheduled me for surgery to open my knee up and removed the other pins. Man, you talking about a relief, I was glad my knee trouble had turned out to be minor. He wrote up a note for me to be off from work for a week. I didn't think I needed the time off, but it sure was appreciated.

Paula had been thinking about her family over the past two months. She wanted to show her adoptive parents our son, but they didn't want to see her, especially the mother, when she had called them. That hurt her feelings, they still didn't accept her marrying a black man. To be honest they were mean to her the whole time she lived with them. The first family she lived with, they used to put her in the chicken shack sometimes, because she was scared of the chickens or for their kicks, sometimes they'd tell her in the morning as she was leaving for school they were putting her bicycle in the trash. Then they'd put it to the sidewalk as she was leaving, then she'd cry and be worried all day at school about her bike and hope they wouldn't put her in the chicken yard when she got back there. Ain't that some mean, sick shit to do to anybody, no less a child? These people mentally and emotionally tortured Paula and her older sister. The people she wanted to see her baby were the second family to take her in. This week off from work would give me time to help her forget about them and cheer her up.

The whole story went like this. Her real father had her mom killed, he thought she was having an affair on him. Then he put Paula, her older sister and younger brother up for adoption. From here the kids bounced around from home to home and the girls lost contact with their brother as little kids, then the sisters lost contact with each other before they reached their teens. She was so young when she lost track of her brother she didn't really know if he existed or was it just a thought far in the back of her mind. For all the mess Paula's been through, she's a strong and sweet person. Most people would be so messed up in the head and heart after the abuse she's been through. She's a good, honest down to earth person after all she's been through, and you think sometimes I've had it rough.

Allen...............

I was right about watching my back at work. This supervisor for some reason was trying to give me a hard time. He and I hadn't had trouble for the last few weeks. He asked me about an empty bottle of liquor that had been found on the job. I told him I didn't know anything about a bottle. Then he started hinting that maybe I had been drinking on the job. I cleaned that shit up right away, telling him I wasn't drinking on the job. Then he gonna insist that I knew who was drinking. I didn't have a clue, but even if I had known, I wasn't going to drop a dime. The supervisor dropped the conversation. I went to get a complaint form to write him up and send it to the union about this nut harassing me. I'd write my complaint up before the week was over and submit it. The week was going kind of fast and I didn't get to write up my form, I had been hanging out two nights and preparing for JoJo to arrive.

The following week came around, this was going to be an easy and a short week. I still hadn't submitted my complaint form, I had slacked off the rush to get it to the union, because my supervisor hadn't been giving me a hard time since he'd left it alone last week. What I had noticed is he was giving a few other folks some trouble.

JoJo came home and this day JoJo and I were setting around his grandfather's house. JoJo's grandparents raised him, so he was staying with his grandfather while he was home. He'd gotten a bowl of canned meat out of the refrigerator, he'd also gotten a box of crackers to go along with the meat spread. We were eating this delicious spread on the crackers having a good time talking and laughing at all the fun times we had. Women loved this black brother, his old flame was on him like white on rice when he returned home. My man was doing good for himself, he was a professional student. I teased him about how he'd get a degree and go right back to school to get another degree. I'd always ask him "Damn man, are you ever gonna get a job?"

While we were still at the kitchen table eating when his grandfather walked in and looked in the refrigerator, asking had we seen the bowl that was in the box, JoJo said, "I got this bowl out of there."

His grandfather turned towards us and said, "I'll be damned, that's the bowl of dog food I'm looking for. Ya'll done ate the damned dog food?"

We were in disbelief we'd eaten half a bowl of dog food and worst than that we thought the shit was delicious. JoJo was like, "What? We ate dog food?"

His grandfather was laughing his ass off, I just said, "That was some good ass dog food."

I left his place shortly after finding out I'd eaten dog food. JoJo was going to visit other folks, so I used this time to catch up on a bit of rest, because we had a lot of ground to cover and time to make up for later.

I had to go to work Wednesday and Thursday and I made sure I got to work, tired or hung over. Things were still cool those two days with the supervisor, though I still had a feeling to beware. I was off Friday as I had requested.

This weekend I saw JoJo for a few hours Friday, he spent time with his ladyfriend and I went by his grandfather's place Saturday around one that afternoon. JoJo was just getting in from the night before. He was leaving Monday morning, he said he was spending this weekend with his grandfather and for me to hang out with them the weekend. I told them I was just stopping by for a minute, they insisted I stay for a while and Grandpa started getting some food together for all of us, not dog food either, but table food. Hours later I headed for home, I was so full. Instead of going home, I changed my mind and headed to my parents house to see them. After I got there and we talked a bit, I took a doze on the sofa and my little sister kept telling me to go upstairs and get in her bed, so I finally did go get in her bed.

It felt good to hear quiet. My sister had painted her room sky blue, white ceiling, with an aquarium that had white and blue gravel in it, she also had a blue light on her wall. It was relaxing, it was supposed to give the feeling of being under the ocean. I laid back looking at the ceiling and glancing at the fish swimming in the tank and before I knew it I had drifted off. I woke up about an hour later, went downstairs, got a sandwich and hung out there for a short while. I left my parents home and went straight home and just relaxed. I took my shirt and shoes off turned on the television and laid across the bed, when the phone rang.

I didn't feel like answering it, but I did. It was Lynn, she wanted to make plans for us to get together, but I didn't feel like making plans right then. I told her I wanted to see her, but I wasn't in a talkative mood right now. She understood, I told her I'd call her back later tonight. She was a sweet chick, but I didn't see our friendship growing into anything. All I could think of at the moment was to get up and scrabble over to the kitchen cabinet to get some scooter pies and grab a glass of milk and lay back down. You know that feeling of "aah" when your body touches your mattress. I ate half the damned box of scooter pies, finished my milk and fell into a hard deep sleep. While asleep something woke me up, it was the doorbell. I forced myself to answer it, it was somebody that had the wrong address.

While I slept, somewhere along my dreams I had a fleeting thought that maybe I'm lonely at times, but my conscious mind told me to take more time to myself.

Marie...............

I had met this guy, that was a little younger than me, we exchanged numbers. He lived around the corner from Monica's babysitter. We'd said hello when we saw each other. He was tall, dark, and handsome, with gorgeous white teeth and he was a sharp ass dresser. Yet he didn't have a car. I had called him we'd had a nice conversation and he convinced me to let him come over. He came over, along with a bottle of vodka, orange juice and the fixing for dinner. Yes, he cooked a delicious meal, pork chops, smothered apples and baked potatoes. I sat at the kitchen table sipping on my cocktail talking and watching how comfortable he was in the kitchen. Desert was butter pecan ice cream. After dinner I was so full, I had two plates of food. We sat on the sofa talking and watching television, he stood up around eight o'clock and said he had to leave, but he'd call me tomorrow. I was surprised he was leaving so early and not even trying to get some. I walked him to the door where we exchanged a nice kiss. I saw and talked to him for a few months before I let him meet my daughter, Roy was a gentleman. Very respectable and always brought a snack for Monica or soda.

Come to find out my friend Linda had dated some guy and this guy knew Roy. Well, Linda's friend told me Roy was a drug dealer. I couldn't believe it, I finally asked him about it. Roy admitted it was true and I told him I couldn't continue seeing him. He understood and as usual was a gentle man about the situation.

About now I was getting tired of the dating scene, from now on it was going to just be casual and friendly dating once in a while. No hassles, I really enjoy men, but don't want their ass around me all the time. There's too much drama and games with them. I don't have the energy to put into the shit anymore. I know men probably say the same thing, but I'm for real about this.
I fixed myself a drink and sat back to watch television and reflect and plan my upcoming week. This was more like it, relaxing, no man stress.

Junie…………..
Time as usual wasn't waiting for anybody. It had been almost two years since we'd had a baby and Paula had missed her cycle this month. We were excited for her doctor's appointment. We had been trying for another baby. God would see that we got along fine. We were struggling, but really who wasn't. Paula always had a nice ample rear, but when she was pregnant it got a bit plumper. I was not complaining, I love a woman with meat on her. Bones need not apply here, nope don't want no bones.

Paula was now in her sixth month when my Uncle Rob past away. He'd had a tumor of the brain, he survived the surgery, but went into shock when he woke up and realized he'd survived it. That's sad. He was such a good man, kind to everybody, easy and a smooth personality. We gave our second born the middle name Robert after him. Our second son was born cute as could be, but with some health problems. Such as a spot on his lung, they had to remove the portion for the lung with the spot. This was a difficult time for us, our baby was in the hospital, he was just an infant. Why was he going through this? Paula and I cried and prayed many a times while he was sick. Thank God our baby survived it all and became very healthy. As the doctor said, he is now thriving, all plump he was, I nicknamed him ChubbyDaddy.

I was working my ass off, doing overtime when it was available, had taken a little time off from school to help with the children and our bills. After three years out of school, I figured I'd better get back to it. Paula had gone back to work this year to help out financially so that I could afford to go back to school.
Her paycheck would makeup for the lack of my overtime or doing gardening work. She was a very supportive wife, in every way and of course my family helped by babysitting anytime. Sometimes they'd keep the boys overnight so we could have some time to ourselves.We appreciated their babysitting and time alone, but by the second day we were glad to go get our babies back.

Time was passing, it was about five years down the road, the kids were growing strong and healthy, I was doing pretty good in school, but there was a slight change in Paula. I'd tried to talk to her about it, but didn't really get anywhere with the conversations. She was not as sociable as she normally had been. It was getting close to a year of this, her staying home instead of visiting family, or not answering the telephone. She said she answers telephones all day at work, that's the last thing she wanted to do at home. I understood her point, but now other people had started mentioning Paula not seeing Paula or hearing from her. Eventually, I told Paula maybe she should see somebody that might be able to help her. Maybe she's suffering from depression. I had my degree in nursing psychology, I was pretty sure she was depressed. She wasn't down for that idea, so I let it slide a while longer. About five more months had passed when I suggested if she went to talk to someone about her problems, I'd go with her. She agreed this time, I was glad. There had been some foul things going on, since her long lost sister had shown up. I mean her natural sister, who she hadn't seen or heard from in over twenty years. Seeing her sister and hearing about some of the awful things that had happened, had caused emotional trauma to her, whether she admitted it or not.

I don't know if her sister meant any harm, or was she a bit touched in the head. Who can truly say, to me it was a little of both.

After seeing a counselor about her mental and emotional state. During this time she'd heard her real father was still alive and her sister took our oldest son to meet his grandfather. Come to find out he was still a part of the mob, so we didn't allow our sons to see him again. Shit that wasn't a big deal to him anyway, he's thrown his kids away, he didn't give a shit about not seeing his black grandsons.

Spending time with her sister seemed to do more harm each visit, Paula eventually stopped associating with her sister. Which I imagine was a hurtful thing to do, considering this was the second time she had to separate from her natural family.

As time went on all these mixed up confused emotions started taking a toll on our marriage. The worst part of it was I really think she didn't mean to harm our marriage, she was maybe somewhat adrift emotionally.

Then it came the time when I had to say it again, we need to see a counselor to try to get through these problems and try to fix things before our marriage falls apart. My marriage, my family meant everything to me. I had cried many times praying and wondering what was happening to us and to her. I wanted us to workout forever.

We started counseling again and even took our kids with us for a few visits, because we were concerned for them too. I couldn't tell anybody what was going on in our house. Was it pride that made me this way? Yes. Was is hurt? Yes. Was it disappointment? Yes.

I did finally to talk to my mother about it all, I was sitting at the kitchen table where most conversations took place. My mom and I sat down and I started telling her all that had been going on. My Mom was at the kitchen sink when I started crying some, I'll be honest I'm a man that's not shamed to cry. We weren't taught that boys don't cry. We were taught you're human, you have emotions there's nothing wrong with crying. I didn't let just any or everybody to see my soft side, because in everyone's eyes, I'm the Prudential Rock, a solid foundation. My brother and I call our youngest sister, the baby, she rubbed my shoulders without saying anything and laid her head on top of my head to comfort me. This was the first time my sister had seen me cry, but I was getting older now and experiencing different situations that were important and emotional to me. When I was younger late teens and early to mid twenties I guess we still have that hard exterior, some kind of shield up, let me tell you as a man if that shield doesn't fade as we grow something's wrong or you haven't been living a meaningful life.

My mom understood what I was saying, yet a part of her got a little mad at Paula for putting me through this. I told her not to be mad at her, she really is having mental and emotional problems.

Eventually, Paula came home from work one evening and asked for a divorce. I lost it. As soon as it came out of her mouth, I slapped her down. I couldn't believe it, that she had said she wanted a divorce or that I had slapped her to the floor. I started asking her to forgive me for hitting her and asking her to think about it for a while, I don't want a divorce. This was a rough night, and I truly mean a rough night, to have built my world around my wife and kids and now for my world to be crumbling down on me.

She didn't change her mind about it though. So being civilized, we planned what we thought was best for our sons, she thought I should keep the boys. Finally, we went to see a divorce lawyer and we couldn't afford to pay him.So he told me if I did the paperwork myself it would only cost me around seven hundred dollars. So I got started on paperwork, driven by hurt and some anger to get it over with.

It seems our boys were able to accept the divorce, but was mostly concerned that they wouldn't be split apart from each other.

Through it all we all survived this ordeal and are hanging in there.

Allen...............

My son had told my little sister he wanted to come spend the weekend with her. She told him yes, so Trina and my mother talked and set the plan in motion. My mother and little sister had drove to my place and Taz came running to my crib to tell me, little Allen was coming to spend the weekend. I was as excited as she was, I grabbed her and gave her a big ole hug. She said, "I told you when he got old enough he'd come to you."

She had a lot of damned wisdom for her age, that's all I could say to myself. She told when he'd be coming, while my mother stayed in the car waiting for her. I walked Taz out to the car and of course to speak with my mom for a few minutes.

That Friday I wasn't at my parent's house when Trina, her new friend and little Allen arrived. I came over later that night. They had left about and hour before I got there. He and I hugged, talked, he was quite a football player, his position was quarterback. He even had a Pop Warner football card like the pros with his picture on it and his stats. I was impressed by my son, he was smart as hell and we had things in common. I didn't stay late, but it was hard to make myself leave. We all kissed farewell as usual and I told him I'd see him tomorrow. I was exited and nervous about seeing my own flesh and blood.

After getting back home to my surprise I did get a decent night of sleep, knowing I'd see him again tomorrow.

The next morning was Saturday, I was still nervous. I got to my parents' house around one that afternoon, trying to play it cool. Before I arrived I had a two drinks to loosen up. He and I got in my car and we rode around visiting family and friends. Everyone was saying how he looks so much like me. To be honest he's just a lighter version of myself.

After this he was talking smack about the basketball court, I had to take his little ass up to the courts so I could school him. The only problem was I had on shoes, not sneakers. So I was slipping a bit on the court. He had game for sure, just like his old man. I won the game, but it was close. We got back to his grandparents' a little after dinner, my brother was there, waiting to see his nephew. We were talking about our game and he had the nerve to challenge me to another game with my sneakers and he'd spot me a few points. I was like no this boy did either. I took him up on it, and he and I set the time for another game Sunday. We were having a good time I said I was going to run to the store I'd be right back. My mom stopped at the back door to tell me not to get anything to drink, I told her I wouldn't, but I did go buy a pinch pint. I didn't get drunk, just a little maybe loosened up.

I told my son I'd be over earlier the next day, in time for breakfast and I then headed for my place about ten o'clock. I was more relaxed, not because of the alcohol, but because he and I had spent some time together and I was getting to know him some. People change over a period of time, especially kids, they're growing and changing every few days. Sunday we stayed around the house, didn't go play ball.

Later the evening his mom arrived to pick him up. She looked good. Damn she looked good. It was nice seeing her and talking, for real. He and I were sitting on the loveseat, she was admiring how much he looked like me, same facial expressions, even to lifting one eyebrow was a natural bewilderment expression for us. She fell out laughing at the two of us together. Then they left heading back to north Jersey. Man, after this first visit he began coming to visit on a regular, this was great.

It was two months later when I worked up the nerve to have my son stay at my place. He usually clung to my little sister. He was glad to stay with me, but wanted to know when Taz was going to pick him up tomorrow. My little sister's not old enough to drive, but I assured him we'd go to my parents' around noon tomorrow. Then he was okay, and we settled in for some TV and eating. Things were going somewhat good between us, but he wasn't comfortable when I'd had a drink. I don't fake the funk, I'm me and don't put on fronts. I told him I would watch my drinking around him and wouldn't endanger him or me. I'd done some stupid shit when I'd been drinking, like calling the police department in rich white towns to let them know I'd be coming through flying, or playing cop, stupid shit like that. I didn't tell him about my silly episodes. I'd gotten better though, I hadn't done that dumb stuff in many years.

Little Allen had been coming to spend the weekends for a few years and it was a Friday I had gone to the American Legion for happy hour, but left in time to pick up my son at my parents' by seven o'clock that evening. I took him to meet a female friend of mine, nothing special was going on between us, but she was good people. We stayed at her house for about an hour and a half. There were some people at the Legion I wanted to see him, so the Legion was our next stop. It was around ten o'clock at night when we got there. He was concerned about going in a bar, I assured him it was alright. "There are some people inside waiting to meet you, they've heard so much about you", I said. They were waiting for him, so we went inside. Most of these people knew him from when he was a baby and hadn't seen him in years. I was feeling proud introducing him around, everyone talking to us and just trying to get a brief update on his life. We had been inside about twenty minutes, then he told me he was ready to leave, we didn't leave right then, I was talking to a few people. He walked toward the restrooms, when he returned to where we were setting, he told me he'd called Taz to pick him up. At this age my sister was now driving, she was there in front of the place within five minutes, I had gone outside to wait with him, I walked him to the car and said I'd be there in a short while. Taz told me to take my time, and to stay out of trouble. They were going to go home and go to bed, she'd leave the back door unlocked for me.

The next day my little sister told me as soon as he got in the car with her, he wanted to know why my father would take me to a bar. She told him he just wanted you to see some people that wanted to see you, he didn't mean any harm although it wasn't the best idea. Now that I was completely sober, I know that wasn't the best idea at that time, but no harm had been done, so I talked to him about it.

I had been so wrapped up with looking forward to spending time with my son, I wasn't even thinking about getting into a relationship with anyone. I just had the casual, yet special friend I had taken him to meet. She was asking for more of a relationship, I was honest with her about my feelings for her. She dug where I was coming from, we continued seeing each other for some time after, but things started fading between us about eleven months after the talk we'd had. One good thing was happening, during the time I'd been seeing my son, I had eased up on drinking some.

My son would be graduating from high school in about three years now, during his early teens he didn't come to visit as much, he was busy chasing girls quite a bit, there was nothing wrong with that, it was normal. I told him about sex and to use condoms if he felt he couldn't resist the temptation of sex. At the age of seventeen, little man got his license and he and his friends would pop into town at any given moment. Sometimes we'd miss each other, but it was good to know he knew his family and had been at the house earlier that day, or to get word that he'd be popping in sometime later that evening.

He invited me along with the rest of the family to his high school graduation, but I didn't go, I went to work that day. It didn't make any sense for me to have missed this day, but for some reason I couldn't get myself to attend. Maybe I felt like I hadn't done enough for him all those years, but he wanted me there anyway. Later that summer he went off to college, this was the best thing he could have done. I always stressed education to him.

Marie...........

I was serious about coolin' out with relationships. It had been a few years since my last real man or boyfriend.

Life had been smooth, no bumps, a date when I felt the need and that was enough. Then one day, I met this joker Jonathan, a Mississippi boy with gray eyes and pecan brown skin, curly black hair, sounds good right? Jonathan always called me Shorty, although I was a few inches taller than him. None of my folks had ever heard of calling women shorties, but I figured it was a southern thang. Well as usual the beginning of the relationship was all stars and fireworks, he was entertaining and a few years younger than me. The family thought he was all right, nothing to write home about, but if I was happy with him, then they were okay with whomever we dated.

Lots of times he'd bring over a bunch of record albums, even though I already had lots of music. My stereo wasn't far from my living room door that led to the porch, so the screen door allowed my music to come out into the yard or I'd put the speakers on the porch. My father cooked on the barbeque pit at least four times a week, so it was like a small cookout damned near every day. Whoever was at our houses sat out in the yard or porch and cooled out. Later in the evening Jonathan and I sometimes went for a ride then would come back to my place for a little romantic action. I was content with the way our relationship was right now.

This morning came and I slept late, it was close to seven a.m. Saturday, when I opened my bedroom curtains, then I went down to the kitchen and opened the curtains at that door. This way everybody knew I was up, especially my mother. This family started our visiting each other early, usually in time for breakfast. My girl Leya came to my door around ten o'clock, I was upstairs vacuuming when she came in the door yelling my name. I turned off the vacuum and went downstairs, she was setting on the floor in front of the stereo tuning into a jazz station. We both walked in the kitchen, I got a glass of juice, Leya fixed herself a cocktail. I was like "Is it that bad, this early in the morning?"

She answered, "No I feel like a drink, goddamnit. Is that alright?"

She seemed like she was fine. So we sat it the table and sipped and talked, this chick kept me laughing as usual. She cursed like it was so natural to her. I swear she was a female Richard Pryor.

While she and I were talking I decided to take me a quick bath and put on a cute little yellow sundress before we proceeded out to the porch. We were out on the porch talking and laughing when my phone rang.

I went inside to answer it, Jonathan was on the other end. He asked me what I was doing, I told him setting outside talking with Leya, he seemed to get a slight attitude because she was here. I asked him if he was coming over, he said no. So I thought to myself if he's not coming over why is he concerned about her being here. I figured, oh so he's a bit jealous, uhm? I guess by our seventh month into seeing each other our time spent together started to lessen, but I didn't say anything because we hadn't agreed to see each other exclusively. We were officially still just dating and hanging out together. Jonathan came over about three days or nights out of the week, most times I cooked not usually for him, because I cooked for my daughter and myself anyway, so he'd eat while he was here. He sometimes gave me money for groceries because he was at my place eating so often.

Junie............

Well, even after our divorce Paula and I remained great friends. My boys were doing really good and so am I to be honest. We've had to adjust our lives, but with the help of my family it's been much easier than I expected.

I finished nursing school so I'm making good money and I started college for alcohol and drug abuse counseling, I found I truly enjoyed this field of work. I'd also met a nice lady that helped me with some of my studies towards the end of my nursing courses, she was diggin' on me, but I didn't feed into at all. I was a gentleman as usual, let her know at the same time romance was not on my mind. When I actually met her I was going through a lot of shit trying to hold onto my marriage. She respected me being married, which made things real smooth between she and I during study time. Although every now and then she still gave subtle little hints that she was attracted to me. I couldn't afford to not have her tutor me at this point. After Paula and I got divorced, I'd say about a year later, I did go on a date with her. It was nothing fancy, we just went out for a pasta dinner and a movie, she was cool. She too was thick with dark coloring and also Italian. Paula was Sicilian, and Lisa was Roman.

I was taking this friendship extremely slow, I made it very clear to her. Every once in a while we'd go out, but she called me kind of regularly just to say hello and to see how me and my boys were doing. She already knew how we were doing, because her son and my son had been best friends for years. She'd invite us over to dinner sometimes, and I will say, she was a fantastic cook, man I mean she could burn. She was kind of known around the neighborhood as the Italian Momma, she always had her kids' friends eating at her house.

After about nine months I broke down and invited her and her kids to my parents for a little cookout, they all hit it off from that day on. Her son had visited my parents house on occasion with me and my boys for several years before, say like for Halloween, or if he was hanging out with us for a few hours. Come to find out, Lisa had talked to my mother about how hesitant I was to get into a relationship and how I had told her I had no plans to get married again. I didn't say anything to her about putting my business out, because I knew my Mom understood my situation and my reasoning. Heck, my Mom and Dad had both told me to take my time, there was no reason to hurry into anything. I needed time to get myself together emotionally and to put my attention towards my boys and me. She admired how close me and my boys were and how well we functioned and ran our home without a woman.

I had been taught to do all the things a woman can do around the house and I was teaching my kids the same thing. We, men didn't need a woman to take care of us or to cook for us, we needed a woman for companionship. Actually, one time Lisa and I were in my kitchen when we had gotten into a little argument about me not needing her for household chores. Finally after she had gone home and thought about our debate, she realized that me not needing her to be my house slave was a good thing. I continued trying to keep our friendship on a slow track, but somewhere, somehow Lisa started bringing up marriage. I was like, "Oh no, not this shit."

After about two weeks of her talking about our relationship being committed and tying the knot, I had to tell her in a nice way, that maybe we shouldn't see each other. Oddly enough she agreed with me. She didn't intend on wasting her time dating a guy that had no intentions of getting married to her. So we stopped seeing each other. I did better than she did on staying away though. I didn't call or go by her place, but she called me about once every two weeks to see how we were doing. I told myself I had to accept that I did miss her, she was a great companion - we enjoyed so many interests, she was a damned good cook – all kinds of food, my boys liked and knew her –

for years before I even knew her, and here's the flincher – maybe I loved her. There I said it, how's that?

Allen.............

I was taking a long hiatus from dating, nothing near steady. Just once in a while to take care of my male desires. To be honest I felt good being on my own, I never really liked answering to anybody about my actions or whereabouts. I was working two jobs now for a short while, enjoying family and once in blue moon taking a drink or a beer, which was a change from how I had been doing for some time. I realized and accepted I had been drinking too much, even acting a fool once in a while, you know getting in stupid situations being intoxicated, but I decided to slow my roll. Also, sometimes to find a special someone, you must first spend time alone to find yourself, so who knows I might profit in more than one way from this.

My son was doing well and he was smart as hell, which we had known since he was a tiny baby. Man, my brother was thinking of getting remarried. Not this kid though, once was enough for me, I'm not joking.

Marie.............

About a year into the relationship Jonathan started showing his ass, running around with other women and lying.

Come to find out he was even married, but separated and seeing his wife too. She let me know she existed, no we're not living together but he spends some nights with me, she had said. I was like what's new he seems to be spending nights with a few different women. I tried to break up with him, but that seemed to make him more persistent at keeping me on his string, but he wasn't leaving the other women alone. Then I'd give in to him, we did this dumb shit for about a year and a half. Then I did stop seeing him, again here comes his wife telling me she's going to get me. He's my husband, she had said. I told her, "Please take the son of a bitch, I want him to stay away from me. But I know you don't think I'm the only one. Please, he was several women, so you need to check them out or better yet, check your run around runaway husband."

I told the poor pathetic woman to get out of my face and not to call my house anymore. That fool had followed him seeing where he went, that's how she found out where I lived and had gone through his pockets and wallet getting phone numbers. I wasn't even mad at her for calling me or approaching me, she was such an emotional mess.

Well, he stopped dealing with the wife and got divorced within the next year. Then he started calling me on the regular and stopping by for a minute here and there. He started growing back on me, so I wasn't minding his company, but I was trying to take things slow. He and I were having a good time together, we hung out around my house all of the time. I think we actually went out twice in about three years. What you think, something doesn't sound right? I was thinking the same thing, but was letting it slide.

After a while I had starting asking him why we never went anywhere, that's odd. He never had a valid reason. I figured he was seeing other women, because John and I only spent a few hours together whenever he came to see me. He never stayed the whole day or evening, if he did spend the night he left first thing in the morning, I'm talking leaving by the time the sun came up. I was feeling like this had become more of a wham bam thank you mame relationship that had gone on for years.

Then I along with a few other people was thinking my best friend Leya was telling this bastard my other business that didn't concern him. Even thinking he was also seeing my best friend, Leya. I was like no that wouldn't happen, she's been my dawg since we were kids. Then again, my Grandmother used to say, "Watch out for friends and family, they're close enough to get to you. Your enemies can't get as close to you." My Grandmother's saying is true for sure.

Time passed and I had to accept that my girl Leya and John were spending time together without me. My little sister was driving now and even she and my daughter thought they were sneaking around, so they had done a drive by Leya's apartment to check for themselves. They drove into the parking lot of her apartment building but didn't see his car, so something told them to park down the street and knock on her door, Leya answered the door, she was fully dressed, she told them to come on in. As they past through her living room to set down, there was John at the kitchen table in the middle of getting his hair cut by Leya. The girls played it cool, Leya told them he had came by to get his hair cut. My sister asked John where do you normally get your hair cut? Then Taz added, Leya is good at cutting hair, but so is my sister. They continued to play the shit so cool. Then Leya offered Taz and Monica a soda while she finished cutting his hair. So they both accepted a soda, because they love soda and they figured this would also give them extra time to see what was up here. Before the girls left, our cousin Dave came by to check out Leya. The two of them, that is, Dave and Leya had been seeing each other for the past about ten months. After Dave arrived and saw John setting at her kitchen table he asked to speak to Leya in the other room, which was her bedroom, she went with him. The girls said Dave didn't seem too happy according to the look on his face when he saw John there. So Taz and Monica casually left just like they casually stopped by. The question was still, is John and Leya having a sexual relationship I couldn't prove it to be yes, but there was something going on. I had to speak to them about it, of course they denied it, but I didn't believe either one of them. Inside I knew he wasn't shit and I'd known her through all kinds of situations. She could be wild, and truly knowing her, I knew for sure she was lying to me. I left both those skanks along.

John would still call me and come by every now and then. Both of them still swearing nothing was going on between them. There's a line that your boyfriend or girlfriend is not supposed to cross or allow the opposite sex to cross in the relationship. Ain't life something?

As time past I kept some distance between two people I had really enjoyed and of one of them had been my partner in crime, my best friend since we were about twelve years old.

To come to this realization hurt and disappointed me a bit. Like my Grandmother had said when I was growing up, "Watch out for friends and family."

Grandma was right about a lot of what she had said, so when you hear older people saying old saying, listen up. John came over trying to keep a spot in my bed, but I was easing him out of my bed and my life. Sometimes he'd come by and I'd talk to him in my living room or kitchen, he'd even asked me one day, why can't we go lay down and relax. I just told him that wasn't such a good idea. John was one of those hot headed types, he would get to fussing and I didn't have enough feelings for him to even get into an argument. I figured he'd come around here a few more times if left up to him before he gave up, but I planned on telling him point blank next time he came over to kiss my ass. Somehow I was enjoying stringing him along for a minute though. You know making him be so sweet, he'd bring me things, even though the things were never anything of any value. Please get real, that cheap ass bastard.

My cousin Bea came by to see me and for me to do her hair, while I was doing her hair and I was sipping on some vodka and orange juice I gave her some of the lowdown and dirt on what had been happening. She always had something to say that made me laugh, I mean a good healthy laugh, yet what she'd say had truth to it. She also said to me, didn't I warn you about your Leya some time back, I told you she was okay, but to keep an eye on her. My cousin and I used to laugh, talk and drink for hours, back when we thought we were so damned cool and just out of high school. Bea had cut way back on drinking some years ago, she took a sip of wine regularly, but she was still up to it when it came to talking and making people laugh their asses off.

A few days had past before John came over again, just like I knew he would. I invited him into the kitchen where I was finishing up some cooking. I had made barbequed ribs, candied yams, green beans and cornbread. He and I were sitting at the table eating and talking, when he brought up that time when I was trying to seduce him, I was dressed in a sexy loungier, cooking a rib dinner. John was eating and telling me how good my cooking was, he was sucking on a rib and licking sauce, when he picked up something small, it was covered in sauce he was nibbling on it, when he realized maybe this ain't no meat. He had said "Shorty, what's this?"
Then he and I realized it was one of my fake fingernails that had come off while I was cooking. I was a little embarrassed and he was a bit disgusted, but kept right on eating. I knew my nail was missing but didn't think he'd find it in his plate. This time when he tried to head toward

my steps upstairs, I told him to come back to the kitchen for a minute, and he did.

I said, "Look I'm not going to bed with you now or in the future. I've been trying to be friendly towards you after all the wrong you've done to me, so I thought I'd cook and we'd share a meal and talk, but then I got to thinking. Why keep being nice, what did being nice do for me? So I thought maybe I should add a little something in the food today, I hope you enjoyed it?"

John started asking, "What you talking about, you put something in the food?"

I said, "Calm down."

He said, "Calm down my ass, you were just sampling a few green beans, while I ate a whole fuckin' plate of food. Shorty, did you put something in the food?"

I walked out onto the porch while he was talking, he tried to grab my arm, I yanked it away. So he followed me outside, where I told him he'd better get off my property before I called the police to get him off. He knew I had family and friends that were on the police force, so he left without raising hell, but he was looking frazzled.

I didn't hear from that fool for almost three months, then he called me. I told Jonathan I was truly through with him and he shouldn't bother to call me anymore. He asked me, "Shorty are you sure about this?"

I said, "I'm sure about this the last time you came over here and even more sure now," then I hung up the telephone.

I was doing my own thing, nothing big, just going out every now and then with a friend or two. Some time had past, I'd say it had been around seven months since I had last seen Jonathan, when I met another guy, named Tim. Tim was a Jamaican, a short, kind of petite guy, nice looking with a nice grade of hair and amber colored eyes, hard working, with a beautiful personality. I explained to him that I had recently ended a long relationship. So he understood I wanted to take it a little slow between he and I. Tim and I talked four times over the telephone over the next two weeks and we'd gone out to eat twice. He told me a friend of his was having a cookout and he would love to have me as his date. I told him I'd like to come and that I would meet him at the cookout.

By now my daughter had grown up, gotten married and moved about forty-five minutes away from home. I was still keeping away from Leya, so I asked my sister if she wanted to go to the cookout, she already had plans for the day so couldn't make it. I should have let her know ahead of time, she probably would have gone with me. Anyway, I was dressed in a cute black and white short outfit, the top was black with white designs in it, white shorts and black sandals. The cookout was only a few miles from my place. When I arrived there were quite a few cars on the block, I had told Tim about what time I would get there. As I started to park my car about half way down the block from where the cookout was going on, Tim showed up at the side of my car on the sidewalk, he was dressed in a tan colored linen short set. He looked nice with his little short self. He was a janitor at the local hospital, but his style was of a man with class, honor, a gentle personality, and pride exuded from his every pore. After I finished parking he walked to the driver side to open my door. Tim gave me a kiss on my lips then on my cheek as we greeted and started walking towards his friend's house. I was impressed that he was really keeping an eye out for my arrival and that he came to open my door and accompany me inside the yard. About three houses away I could hear the music pumping, it sounded like they were having a good time back there. As we went into the yard he introduced me to folks, most of them had a plate of food or drinks. They were cooking all kinds of foods grilled seafood, steaks, goat, chicken, and it all smelled so good, I got hungry instantly. As we worked our way through the yard meeting people, Tim fixed me a drink at the bar that was set up in the backyard. No alcohol was in the punch, it was a fruit punch drink he made me. Tim didn't drink or smoke. I had to give it to whoever made the punch it was out of this world, bursting with fruit flavor. It would have been even better with some vodka in it though. I knew if he and I were to become a real couple I'd have to cut back on the smoking and drinking. Those were two of my favorite hobbies, it would be hard to do, but he might be worth it. I wished my sister had come, she would have enjoyed this, I thought to myself.

Tim introduced me to his friend that was giving the cookout, as soon as Tim introduced us, his friend asked me to dance. He was already swaying to the music as he asked so I didn't want to be rude, I looked to Tim to see if he minded. He handed my hand to his friend and off we went to dance. We danced through one song, then he returned me to Tim. By this time Tim had made a heaping plate of food. As soon as I got to him, he had a fork full of food heading towards my mouth. I obliged and opened my mouth like a baby bird. The food was absolutely delicious, so flavorful. He found us a couple of chairs to sit in and we shared the plate of food, watching people and talking and laughing. He was so easygoing, and very considerate. I wasn't even used to this kind of guy anymore, but I was making the adjustment to him easily and quickly.

I had finished my punch and gotten rid of the cup, when Tim led me to the dance area. He was a good dancer, real smooth and sensuous. He placed his arm around my waist as we swayed together then he pressed himself against me. It felt pretty nice, it was done in a way that let me know we wouldn't mind being sexual, but not in a way that it was disrespectful. We danced a few songs, before he suggested we get another drink, this time he fixed me a cocktail. I was glad I accepted his offer to come, I was having a nice time. I stayed about another hour before both he and I left. He started walking me to my car, as we reached the front yard two men stopped him to speak for a minute, I told Tim to go ahead and talk I could make it to my car and for him to call me later tonight, he gave a kiss and sent me off. As I approached my car there were two girls leaning on the hood of my car. As I got closer I told them to get off my car, they acted like they had an attitude and was a bit reluctant to get off my car. So I said it again in a more forceful tone. They got off the car and one girl started talking shit to me, I toughened up immediately. I wasn't one to start shit, but I sure could bring it to an end. When they saw I wasn't scared of them they slid their ass away from me and my car. By this time Tim had reached me, asking if everything was okay. "See, I should have walked you to your car," Tim said.

I told him, "It's fine. Just give me a call later."

"Maybe I should see you home sweetheart", he said.

I was smiling and giggling a tiny bit, saying, "Well maybe you should."

He opened my door and waited for me to start the car and turn on the AC, then he said wait right here I'll follow you home.

I realized he was serious about seeing me home, so I stopped him and convinced him I would make it just fine. He knew I'd get home fine, he was just a sweet guy.

Allen.............

As for me things were going pretty smooth, no real bumps in the road. I had gotten me another hoopty, my paychecks were pretty good and steady and so were the flow of women. Nothing serious as far as a relationship was happening. I had hooked up with one chick that we seemed to be a more steady thing, she had a son. Her name was Dee, she and I spent some quality time together kind of often. She was an easygoing type, not demanding, very understanding. I brought her and her son over to meet my parents, not that it was serious or anything, but thought they should meet. My mom said she was nice, my father said she was nice, but I could do better. I probably could do better, but she was good for right now. She drank a little, liked staying home and cooking, kept an immaculate house and was a nurse. Dee looked older than she really was, and was very thin, like model thin. Every now and then she and I would swing by my folks' house to check them out. Nothing eventful went on between the two of us, until one evening about eleven months into seeing her, she had the nerve to ask me where was our relationship going. I was honest and told her I didn't know, because I had no plans to take it anywhere, but I did enjoy her company. She had the nerve to get mad at my answer, so she and I exchanged words and discussed the matter, then she decided maybe we shouldn't see each other, she wanted a growing relationship that would lead to marriage. I got up off the sofa and got the hell out of dodge with a quickness.

About four weeks had past before I heard from Dee again, she showed up at my door one afternoon, wanting to talk. I let her in to hear what she had to say. She went on talking about the relationship we had and how she still thought it had the potential to grow into more. She was a sweet woman, but it was just that I didn't want to get remarried at this point to her or anybody else. To be honest I didn't think I'd ever remarry, because my heart was still belonging to Trina in some kind of way. I didn't tell her about all of this.

Then she reached for my shoulder to rub it, then she moved her hand to my chest as she sat down next to me on my sofa. I felt a little uncomfortable, yet getting turned on some too. Then Dee kissed me softly on my lips, I didn't respond, so she kissed me again, this time I kissed her back a bit. Dee started rubbing my thigh and I knew we shouldn't be doing this, because it would give her the impression of rekindling our relationship, which wouldn't be the right thing to do. I did care about Dee, but not the way she cared for me and I knew it just wouldn't be fair to her to go through with it. Don't get me wrong I was getting turned on, but sometimes you have to know when sex can cause trouble or confusion and convince yourself to not let sex get in the way by saying no and taking a cold ass shower instead. You see eight out of ten times I'd say women can't distinguish sex from making love, that's where shit can get turned into a mess or somebody's feeling getting hurt.

Junie............

I told Lisa that I loved her and I accepted her ultimatum of marriage. It was a cold cloudy day in January when she and I along with our four kids went to the justice of peace to tie the knot. We had on nothing fancy, she had on a light cranberry colored dress, I had on a pair of dress slacks and shirt with a tie, as for the kids they had on whatever they were wearing when they came home from school.

We got married, then went home to our own apartments, we had gone through all the drama of buying a house, we had packed our apartments up to move, so the next day we all moved into our new home. We'd found an oversized ranch house that supplied all the living space we needed both inside and outside and we were just able to afford it, with the help of Lisa's mother. Seems Lisa was so excited about moving she had forgotten to tell her son, that when he got out school to come to the new house instead of going back to the apartment. Well, he got out of school as usual and went home to his apartment to find it bare. He said he was thinking to himself, where the hell did they go, what's going on? They moved and left me, then he thought, "hey my stuff is gone too". So he made his way to the house we had all gone to see when we showed him the new house. He said when he saw the cars in the driveway, he was relieved to see the cars, then a happiness came over him as he picked up speed jogging to the house. Having a new home, a house with a big yard, with my family including my best friends and my new dad, he was thinking.

For the next week we unpacked and settled in, Lisa had invited our families over for dinner to celebrate our marriage and the new home. My girl had cooked up an Italian storm, pasta, sausages with pepper and onions, braggioli, garlic bread, salad, and we had a small wedding cake for dessert. This actually started a family tradition of our family getting together almost every other weekend for dinner and sometimes we'd get together during the week to eat a family meal, even if it was a little something just thrown on the grill. Our family was already known for doing things and going places in packs, yes we traveled in packs like wolves, but we were referred to as the Clampits (as in the Beverly Hillbillies).

Marie............

Three years ago, I hadn't been feeling my best when my daughter got married, I signed myself out of the hospital two days before her wedding, promising to continue to take my medicines. Of course I continued taking my medication, I was being treated for pneumonia. Pneumonia was nothing to play with.

It was now early September around a few weeks after Labor Day when I started feeling a bit run down. I went on each day with my regular routine, spending time with my family and friends and with my new bou Tim. I had cut back on my drinking some and was trying to cut back on smoking, because Tim didn't drink or smoke. He was short and sweet and worth the effort to cut back on these unhealthy habits. My family was glad I was cutting back on the liquor and cigarettes. I have to tell you Tim was a short man, very nice looking with a tight little body, but not everything on him was little, if you know what I mean. Don't forget he is a Jamaican, I don't know if Jamaican men lived up to the myth, but Tim did. He was patient, tender, passionate and well hung. To be honest I always thoroughly enjoyed sex and when it came time for Tim and I to get it together I always looked forward to it, smile.

Monica was going through an unhappy time in her marriage, but was trying with her husband to make the marriage work. he may have been trying more than her husband to make the marriage work to be honest.

My relationship was coming along nicely, sometimes Tim and I would go out to dinner, a movie or dancing, but his favorite was going to the beach to relax, then there were times we'd stay around home watching television, playing cards/board games and talking. He made me know he didn't just want me for sex, he always made sure I knew he enjoyed everything about me, I felt so appreciated and cared for with him. It had years since a man made me feel like this. Monica would come down most weekends with or without her husband to spend the day or weekend.

I was going out Halloween night for dinner with a few friends from work, I had told my mother I was feeling really tired, but I was still going because I wouldn't be out late. My friends and I met at the restaurant and it was full, a lot of people were dressed for Halloween and the atmosphere was fun and festive, the food uhm delicious. I've always enjoyed good food and this place sure knew how to serve it up. I had a drink with dinner, vodka and orange juice my usual.

After returning home or to my parents house by eight-thirty p.m., I talked about how much fun I'd had, the good food and how some people dressed in costume had been acting a fool, then I went home to get some sleep.

It was Thursday night, just one more workday before the weekend, thank goodness.

The weekend came, Friday night Tim had to work, so we talked on the phone off and on all evening and part of the night, he said he'd come over the next morning as soon as he got off from work. I fell asleep for the night without Tim calling me again after one, thirty in the morning. I've always been early to sleep and early to rise, most times I'd be sleep by nine o'clock at night. Tim got to my place real early, I opened the door to let him in, he had a little bouquet of three flowers for me. A red, a yellow and a white flower, I was surprised at him. We kissed as he entered, I thanked him for the flowers as he headed for the living room, I asked him if he wanted anything. He just wanted a cup of tea and two toasts before he took a nap. I fixed his tea and toast while he had gone to my bedroom and removed his clothes before coming back to the kitchen to get his food. His little light brown body was very toned, he looked like he took care of himself and he looked good. He told me to go lay down, I looked like I didn't feel good. I went got in the bed, when he returned to the bedroom, he had made me some mint tea and had two aspirin for me to take. Then he joined me in the bed and turned on the television, we talked, and cuddled bore he fell asleep, I slept for another thirty minutes maybe, before I eased out of bed and downstairs. I watered my plants, mopped the kitchen floor and did some dusting before settling down on the sofa with a cigarette and calling my mom and Aunt Kate. Monica and I had talked last night so I knew she wouldn't be coming down this weekend, but she called me this morning just before noon, she said in case me and Tim needed some special time to ourselves. She was so fresh. Tim woke up a few hours later, hungry. He decided maybe we should order out for lunch, so we ordered Chinese food, he'd go pick the food up and run by his place to get some things to keep him busy through the day and night before he had to go back to work tonight. Tim returned with a large bag of food, a book to read, some papers, and fresh underwear.

The weather was already cold, but the temperature must had dropped another eight degrees, it was cold and breezy, so we settled in pretty much for the rest of the day. Later this night Tim left for work next day was Sunday, Tim didn't come over, but we talked over the phone, we talked every day.

The following Thursday my daughter came to see me, because I wasn't feeling good. I had gone to the doctor a few weeks earlier and was put on medications for sinus and upper respiratory infection. I told her to stay home, but she insisted on coming down. When Monica arrived my mother and sister were checking in on me. Monica, Taz and a girlfriend of theirs were talking about going out of town for the weekend, going to visit a friend of theirs before the winter weather set in.

So this was the weekend of their trip, so she had brought her weekend bag for her trip to visit a girlfriend in the D.C. area. After she arrived and saw I was able to move around the house even if I was getting around slow. Monica decided not to go away with my sister and their friend, she thought she should stay with me the weekend, but again I convinced her to go to Washington to enjoy her weekend. Monica told me she'd think about it, in the meantime she went to her old room to lay down and watch television. Tim stopped by on his way to work to see how I was feeling, he brought me a huge plate of Jamaican food he had cooked, I didn't have much appetite, but I had to get some of that food in my mouth. He was a good cook I had to give it to him. Tim hung around for about an hour and a half before he left for work. Friday morning I was feeling better, still tired though. Monica and I laid around the house relaxing all day, we talked about her marriage, which she wasn't one hundred per cent happy with, but was trying to make it work, she was optimistic that it would get better. Then Friday evening my sister got off from work and came over to see how I was doing and see if they were going to DC, Taz said I looked better today and told me to make sure I take all my medicine, drink lots of fluids and to cancel my hair appointments for the weekend. I was ahead of her on that thought, I had already cancelled my hair appointments this morning, for the weekend.

We all decided they should go away this weekend, so Taz went home for a while and when she returned she had her luggage with her and my mother. My mother assured Monica she would keep a close eye on me. I told her Tim will be here again later tonight on his way to work, my cousin Dave was coming in a little while, he'd be spend the weekend with me.

With all the people that would be around, she felt comfortable with these arrangements and they left for DC late that evening.

I laid on the sofa with a small sip of orange juice and watched television waiting for Tim to show up and as usual he kept his word, he was a good man. After he arrived we went upstairs to my bed, I was feeling too tired for sex, but we cuddled and he rubbed my back which put me to sleep. As I dozed, Tim told me he'd lock the door when he left and he'd see me tomorrow afternoon.

It was a beautiful Saturday morning when I woke up, I was feeling a bit sick again today, nauseous and weak. I opened my kitchen curtains and before I could set down my mother was knocking at my door. I slowly made it to the door to let her in. We talked and she made coffee and as usual she had brought her pocketbook with her to work on her checkbook and write out bills. She made me a light breakfast of a scrambled egg and toast to go with the coffee, I forced it down, while we talked and she worked on her checkbook balancing.

While we were still at the table Dave came downstairs, he was playing my weekend nurse. "Uhm, a nigga, I mean your nurse can't get no breakfast around here", he asked playing. My Mom said, "Just a minute David, let me make your something to eat."

"I'm just kidding Aunt D, I'll make me something," he replied.

Dave got to cooking while my Mom finished up balancing her checkbook and we talked and laughed as usual. My cousin was so darn funny without even trying, he's just a character. By the time Dave was coming to the table to eat his breakfast, Momma was packing her oversized pocketbook so she could go back home. She said she'd see us a little later as she walked out the door.

Nothing special went on this day, Tim came over for a while, he was working overtime tonight, so he came during the afternoon and stayed until he had to go to work. Tim and Dave enjoyed cooking so they spent hours in the kitchen working on some recipe they were cooking up, the house smelled so good. When they finished cooking I called my mother and father to come over for dinner.

My father must have been on his way before my mother even hung up the phone. The guys hung out in the kitchen, while my mother and I ate in the den. We could hear them swapping cooking lies, I mean cooking stories and recipes.

My parents didn't stay long after they ate; they wanted me to go to rest on that delicious meal we'd just eaten. I took their advice and made it up the stairs to bed, I was out of breath going up the stairs. I could still hear Dave and Tim telling wild stories and laughing so loud it made me want to go back downstairs to join them, but I didn't. Before Tim left he came up to check on me and give me a good night kiss, uhm so sweet and tender was his kiss. I slept pretty sound this night, I'd enjoyed my day and had a full belly to sleep on.

Sunday again I wasn't feeling good at all, I felt so weak I told Dave. Dave tried to get me to eat a piece of fruit and drink a cup of tea, but I couldn't force anything down. I felt sick to my stomach, so I sat down on the sofa and kept still. A little while later I told Dave to help me to the bathroom I think I have to throw up. He held me by my arm to help me to the toilet where I threw up, as I was walking out the bathroom I remember passing out. Dave caught me before I hit the floor, then he placed me on the sofa and called my mother to come right away, "Marie has passed out", he told her, "I'm calling an ambulance right now."

The ambulance took me to the hospital and I was admitted right away into the emergency room. The doctors in the emergency room found I had pneumonia and my throwing up had made it spread through out my system. Dave stayed at the hospital while my mother went back home to call Monica and Taz to come back home because I was very sick. Honestly I wasn't just sick but I was unconscious.

Monica was in the shower when the call came in, so Taz talked to Momma and got the news. Taz told their friends what was going on, but didn't want them to tell Monica the whole story so she wouldn't be too upset. When Monica came out the shower Taz told her I was in the hospital so we should go home as soon as she got dressed. She didn't tell her I was unconscious and on life support.

When they arrived at the hospital, Taz told Monica I was not doing that great so don't expect her to be setting up in bed or talking, she had to prepare her for what she was about to see. Taz finally told her that I was unconscious and that I could hear whatever we say to her, so be positive. I knew they both walked into my room, but I couldn't respond to them the way I wanted, I responded by squeezing Monica's hand and fluttering the eyelids to Taz and Monica talking to me and touching me. My Momma and Poppa walked into the room and they were all talking and praying, touching me, rubbing me and asking me to get well. During this time in the hospital I had a lot of family visiting me and hanging around the visitors waiting room. I thought I heard two nurses saying that my family, cousins included were filling up the seats in there and they needed to get additional chairs for my family. During this time Monica stayed at the hospital for days, Taz was here up until Friday night, she went home until Saturday morning, my parents had gone home with her.

Taz could often since death, even if she didn't acknowledge it or if she didn't know who that bad feeling was aimed towards. Friday night while in bed saying her prayers and praying to God make me get well. She said it came to her, that feeling that she would have to let go of her sister, because she had a feeling her sister wouldn't be here much longer. Taz went to sleep and got up early the next morning, washed her hair and told our parents to let's get ready to head to the hospital now. She told them to hurry, she wanted to get there as soon as possible. Momma and Poppa were dressed and ready. They were walking out the house, when the telephone rang, it was Monica calling to tell them to come to the hospital right away, that my blood pressure was dropping. They arrive almost immediately, we lived only three or four blocks from the hospital. When the arrived the nurses and doctors had been doing things to try to get my blood pressure up, but it seemed what they were trying was failing. This Saturday the four of them rotated staying in the room with me, they spent the day patiently as usual. Monica and Taz were rubbing me, when Taz said to Monica, "Marie never wanted to be on life support and at some point we'll have to respect her wishes. I had a feeling last night that we'll have to let her go. Let her know we love her and will miss her beyond belief and we will see her again, she needs to know this so she can go in peace." Then Taz told Monica she was going to get Mommy and Daddy. When she returned my parents were with her and they were crying. They were telling me they loved me, and it was all right if I needed to go, but to go with God and that we'll be together again.

After they reaffirmed their feelings and told me to go with God and prayed for me my blood pressure dropped a bit more. Monica asked the nurse to take the life support off of me, she'll be fine she told the nurse. The nurse and doctor removed the equipment off me and I continued to breathe on my own for a minute as my blood pressure steadily decreased, decreased down to zero over zero. As I arose out of my physical body I could see the four of them were still touching me and crying softly. I could also see Tim walking downstairs towards the elevator to come up to my room as he usually did while he was on duty, but he came to sit with me even when he wasn't at work. As Tim approached my room the nurses at the desk stopped him and told him they would have one of the family members come out to speak to him. Taz came to the desk to tell Tim that I had past away, for a moment he was in shock. He stood there with a blank look on his face yet his mouth was hanging open, then Tim asked her, "What are you saying?"

Taz told him what had happened and he turned red and started to cry, he asked the nurses if he could please go in to see me. Taz said he should come in, and the nurses allowed him in my room. As I looked down, I thought for a second, that's my body down there, I'm out of my body, will I return to it. Then with that thought, I soared up and out of the building and I seemed to be flying at the speed of light, but everything I viewed was very cleared as it past me or as I past it. I saw so many places, people, faces I hadn't seen in a long long time, I saw happy events and gatherings, times from when I was a little girl then all of a sudden I was back at the hospital room looking down on my family and Tim as they finally walked out the room and went into the waiting room, then I felt so light as I seemed to soar straight up and seeing what was going on in the hospital getting further and further from my sight. Somewhere else and somebody else, another presence had gotten my attention and yet I didn't feel afraid.

Allen............

I couldn't get myself to go to the hospital, but I was upset about my big sister being sick and I always kept updated and sent her messages by family members. I called my parents house to see if anybody was home before I went by there. My mom answered the telephone and told me to come over as soon as I got a chance, I told her I was on my way. When I arrived my brother and his family was there, along with Aunt Kate and a few other cars. As I walked in I sensed right away something was terribly wrong. My brother walked towards me as I came into the house and Mom was coming from the kitchen towards me, my brother put his hand on my shoulder as Mommy approached me and she said Marie had past away. I started crying right away, I was like this can't be, but I accepted the reality and went upstairs to be to myself for a short while, but Junie came upstairs within a minute to join me. A few minutes later I came back downstairs, as I entered the den Aunt Kate came to meet me asking if I was alright, I gave her a big ole hug and told her I was okay. This was just hard to swallow.

As we all talked, answered questions and reminisced about old times, people were pouring in the front and back doors, some had bags of food and soft drinks.

Again I had to go sit on the sofa for a minute to let this soak in, Marie my sister being gone. The next few days were a bit fuzzy to me, maybe like being a bad dream. Me and my sister Taz were feeling like a crazy dream was going on.

Monica and my parents made all the arrangements for the funeral. It seemed they were going through the motions but weren't all there. My sister's viewing and funeral service were being held at the funeral home instead of the church, because none of us were thinking in our right mind. The night of the service the funeral home was over run with people, the lobby and the outside yard and sidewalk were full of people for the services.

The day following the funeral I went to work just going through the motions and I also figured it would help to take my mind off this. A few days had past, I decided to head to a local bar for a drink or two, to give myself a break from thinking about what had just happened to our family. I guess going to work kept me a little busy, but it didn't stop me from thinking about Marie. While in the bar I ran into a few friends and cousins, had a couple of dances and drinks, I ended up staying longer than I thought I would, but I enjoyed myself. I'm telling you things happen, it's a part of life, it just keeps carrying on.

That following year my Aunt Kate past away, she had been like a mother to my siblings and myself. Our family took another hard hit with her passing. To be honest people on both my father's and mother's side of the family had been passing away really often. You know the old saying, "death comes in threes", will it was about right for us.

I had stopped drinking, maybe two or three times a year I might have a beer or a mixed drink. My job was going good, I had decided to change my job field. I was enrolling to become a truck driver, I liked tractor trailers, but my sister Taz told me she wouldn't allow me to drive across country alone, I'd have to do local runs. I could only be gone over night once in a while, if not she'd had to be my driving partner. She was serious when she told me this.

I signed up for truck driving school and while waiting to start school I had began looking into buying a condo or townhouse. I didn't want a house because I didn't want to deal with taking care of the yard and a townhouse or condo just seemed like less work. One day while at my parents', we discussed my choice for a condo and not a house, they agree it made sense, but said remember it'll be like living in an apartment with neighbors, but with the townhouse I'd have a small yard at least.

So I found a realtor and she started the search to find me a place. I kept my options open, I agreed to look at both condos and townhouses.

It was July, a hot July I might add, as usual on the weekends there'd be family and cousins over to my parents' house that was the hang out spot. They had a pool table, full bar in their home, and a big in-ground swimming pool with two grills outside, a gas grill and a beautiful grill my Pop had built. So it was the fourth of July this day when I stopped in on them, I had my newspaper with me, to glance over while I was relaxing in front of the television, I wasn't expecting the yard to fill up with family this day. I figured the young ones had friends they'd be visiting. When I arrived there were two cousins along with Taz and Monica in the pool out back, they were having a ball. I sat where I could look out the window overlooking the patio and pool. Mom, Pop and I were talking, Pop was making a stew today, as hot as it was outside. Before I could get into reading my paper, people were popping in, bringing bags of food and drinks. Taz and Monica had gotten out the pool to turn on some music and start the gas grill, then my cousin Millie came in the door, she was a lot of fun, she was more my age. She sat at the dining room table with me, Pop had started making his stew. When he said he was making a Brunswick stew some folks said, a stew as hot as it is today. Pop went on putting stuff in the big pot.

By three o'clock the yard was full of people, music, laughter and food, so we went outside to join the fun.

I kept a pair of shorts at the house, because I'd been known to jump in the pool seven o'clock in the morning, before people in the house were even awake, so I was prepared.

Well, after the stew was ready, everybody was waiting to get a taste of it, because everyone knows my Pop can burn. The Brunswick Stew was out of this world, we loved it.

I left earlier than most of the others did, but Millie and I had agreed to meet later at the legion. As I pulled off, Taz was near the fence in the backyard watching me drive away. That night we all parted some folks went to see the fireworks, and I met Millie at the American Legion for a beer and a dance. There were always people you knew there, it was a local hangout, I stayed a little over an hour before I headed for home, but I'd had a really good time all day. Tomorrow the job would be waiting for me, so I headed home to get ready for the workday and get some rest.

The next day as I got ready for work I realized I couldn't find my sunglasses, on the way to work I stopped my parents' I figured I'd left them there. Mom met me at the front door, my Pop had gone somewhere, Monica was in her bedroom watching television and Taz was at work. I told Mom I'd talk to her later as I pulled the front door shut to leave for work after not finding my shades there.

I arrived at work on time, a little while after arriving at work I had to go into the back area, it was hot back there. I needed to bring something out to complete the job order, while I was back there, I felt a sharp pain in my chest and I fell to the floor. I must have laid there about ten minutes before someone else came to see what was taking me so long.

I felt light as if I could float. It seemed like by now I was watching a play take place in front on me, my body laid there on the floor with a gentle smile on my face, as I watched on. I'd had a massive heartache and past with no warning, on the job. According to the doctors and my autopsy, I had died before I hit the floor.

Just when I was really getting my self together, it was time to leave this place and the people I loved so much, there were a lot of people I loved on the other side to see too. Over the last few years I had mellowed some, I take it God had mellowed me as I'd gotten a bit older, prepared me for this time when I would meet him, without me even realizing how I had been changing, yet others who knew me had noticed my change.

Junie............

My brother had all his business together and prepared, insurance and all the necessary papers were easy to find, his will had been made out, everything prepared. I couldn't believe so many of my immediate family were passing away, now my baby brother. That's what Marie and I used to call him when we were growing up to irritate him, we was always trying to be grown, so calling him baby brother would get to him so.

My eldest son sometimes reminded me so much of my brother by acting so much like my brother, I would slip and call him by my brother's name. My family and I had survived Allen's death and were some how moving on with our every day life. It's funny how you miss loved ones, and the older you get the faster it seems time passes. Eventually years had past, and I could still see all my late loved ones as clear as day in my mind, I'm talking about loved ones such as Grandma and Grandpa who had been gone for almost thirty-five years.

Well, things were going really good with the new marriage. To be honest, I was very happy and so were the kids and Lisa, even our dogs got along great. We all had a lot in common, so we did a lot of things together and quite a bit of traveling, like day trips. I'd always been one to get around, to me there was always something to see and some place to go. Time was passing fast, our house had truly become a home for us and our visitors with our frequent get togethers, or meals going on at a minutes notice. Of course, he had big bills to pay monthly, but we were making it and having a good time.

Days turned into months, months into years the next thing I knew me and the ole girl(Lisa), were not having any marital problems.
Along with my ex-wife and I remained great buddies, she was a fantastic person she just had gone through problems, and couldn't seem to accept the help to help bring her out of her troubles. Lisa's daughter had been messing with drugs and we were trying to straighten her out for some time, seems like for a week or two she'd do better, then get a little worse than she was before. I was a drug and alcohol counselor so I had experience dealing with this sort of thing, but she was different. The people I dealt with came to me, because they wanted help getting better, but with her she wasn't coming for help we were trying to convince her to get help and it wasn't working. After more than a year of trying to help someone that didn't want help at that point, I settled back to let things run their course and just be support for Lisa.
Even through all the drug related turmoil her daughter was going through Ami never strayed away from the family, she was always around several times a week and at family gatherings Our boys were doing pretty good, no major trouble from them.

I was feeling pretty well, no real health problems, but it was time for me to have a check up. Close to two years ago I'd had a stress test done and it was fine.

Lisa made my doctor appointment and when the date came we both went for my check up, afterwards we went to lunch by the ocean and then went by my parent's house. We told them about my test and that I would hear the results within two days.

I'd gotten the test results back and the doctors said I had a blockage in an artery and instead of doing a heart bypass, they were suggesting I have angioplasty to clear the blockage. I notified my family and friends, seems everyone was waiting with baited breath to find out.

I had told myself the surgery shouldn't be a big deal, I had the best cardiac surgeon in the area and he'd done heart surgeries on quite a few people in my family and they'd had no problems Everyone seemed to be a bit upset about the news, people were coming by my house to see me and talk to me before my day stay surgery.

George, my best friend came by this one evening when he got off from work to see me, we talked and laughed, discussed my angioplasty, and he said he'd see me later and off he went. He got home and after thinking about me for a while, he got back in his car and drove all the way back to my house to tell me, "I've never said this to anyone before, but I had to come back to tell you I love you."

I was surprised as hell at him saying this, because he was type of guy that covered up his emotions. It felt good to have my buddy open up after twenty-five years of knowing each other.

The next day George had come by earlier that day to check me out, we discussed the surgery, cars and everything else that was going on in our lives. While he was in my driveway, my parents and younger sister pulled up. My brother and I had known George for over twenty-five years; yet this was his second time meeting the family.

He gave everyone a hug of greeting, and really enjoyed hugging my sister; he found her to be quite attractive and liked the feel of her ample breasts when he hugged her. After a while George left and headed home.

My family and I went inside to set down in the living room to discussion our plans and what time we'd meet to go to the hospital, also my Mom was cooking me lamb shanks for dinner Sunday.

My father had been retired for over twenty years, my mother worked part-time; the plan was while Lisa was at work my father would come to my place every day to keep an eye on me. I would enjoy him spending the days with me, we always had a lot to talk about, we liked hunting, fishing, admired nature and he was a good cook and so was I. My eldest son was overseas and the youngest son had returned home from the military a few weeks ago, he was out every day pounding the pavement looking for employment. My boys had become brilliant, caring young men, if I say so myself. I was confident that he'd find a good job soon. My youngest had said he'd stay home for the next few days to take care of me, but I knew my father would enjoy helping out.

After my family and I had talked and hugged as usual, we are a huggy, kissy family they left.

Sunday early afternoon we piled into my parent's house ready to eat, the food smelled so good we could smell it before we got in the door. Mom was in the kitchen putting on her finishing touches while I went into Dad's study to talk and watch television for a while. Taz came to the door to tell Dad and I the food was ready, talking in a Jamaican accent, she was always doing some sort of accent, nobody knows why, she just does.

We gathered at the table with our full plates and said our grace and gave thanks to God before we dug in. After we'd eaten my and Lisa's kids left shortly after the meal, then Lisa and I left earlier than we normally did, because I was scheduled for surgery tomorrow morning, had to be there by seven o'clock.

We all met Monday morning in the admitting area, most people don't have an entourage with them, but like it was said earlier we traveled in packs.

It was time for me to go in for my procedure, of course I was a bit nervous inside, yet I remained as calm as I possibly could. A few hours later after the angioplasty I was wheeled to the recovery room for them to exam me before I was released to go home. As I was wheeled past the waiting area, where I'd left my family they all were still there waiting, they saw me immediately and headed towards me. The nursing staff stopped their stampede and told them to wait so they could get me settled in and then someone would come to bring them in to me. They waved and blew me kisses as I was taken away. A short while later they were brought in the room, as soon as my son saw I was okay he left to go take care of some business.

About an hour later the nurse asked me how was I feeling, I told her pretty good, but I felt a slight pain in my chest. As I kept telling each of them the same thing as they asked me, they decided to do a test to maybe see why I was having discomfort. After bringing me back to my recovery room another nurse asked me if I was still feeling any pain or discomfort. I told her yes, and then she wanted me to rate the pain from one to ten, of course ten being the highest level of pain and one being the lowest, I told her I'd rate it about five to seven. The nurses kept saying there was nothing wrong according to the results, saying I was suffering from anxiety, for me to try to relax and try to imagine I was at a beautiful place somewhere I liked to go to for relaxation. I imagined Bermuda that was one of my favorite places; meanwhile my blood pressure hadn't stabilized since my surgery, now my pressure had dropped low. The blood pressure was fluctuating too much, my sister, wife and mother insisted there had to be something wrong, because I was a calm person, never anxious by nature. Finally my surgeon came in to check on me, he and I had discussed our love of Corvettes, when my sister re-entered my room, I was telling my sister about our conversation and how many corvettes he had. He wanted he and I to get together when I was back on my feet, so the doctor and I were looking to get together about two weeks from today. He'd be seeing before two weeks, he'd be doing my check-ups, but we'd set a time to talk and look at Corvettes. In the mean time, my surgeon also insisted everything was fine; there were no complications, yet I was still having this pain in my chest area.

Well, before the afternoon was over they decided to keep me over night, I convinced my wife, sister and mom to go home, they agreed to go get some rest. I got some rest as well after they left. I woke up around nine that night to find Taz and Mom were setting at the foot of my bed. Taz had spoken to the nurse about my pressure and pulse. Finally the nurse got tired of her mentioning my monitor and came in the room and disconnected it, this didn't stop Taz, and she'd look behind the nurse's station to check my monitor reading. She was telling the nurse my blood pressure and pulse were still not normal, the nurse was becoming agitated, but my sister was right. When my sister came back into the room I told her and Mom I was feeling real warm. So, Taz went to tell the nurse how I was feeling, thinking he'd come to check my temperature. Instead the male nurse came into my room and opened the window right next to my bed, opened it all the way. My mother told Taz to close the window it was too much cool air making a draft on me, and she was right. Another nurse came back to the nurse's station they both told her I was doing fine and although the readings were not yet normal, I had stabilized.

Taz and my mother must have bought it, because my readings were more consistent even if not normal yet, so they left close to eleven o'clock that night to get some sleep.

I knew they'd be back first thing in the morning to take me home.

Through the night I started having difficulty breathing, like I had asthma, not a clear breathing passage, so the nurse called my wife to come to the hospital and bring my medications. Lisa got right up, showered, got my meds together and came straight to the hospital, the whole time wondering why they wanted her to bring medicines to the hospital, when every medication I needed was in the hospital. When Lisa came into the room, she told the nurse she needed to speak with him, they stepped out of the room. Lisa told him, "Look, something is wrong with my husband. His coloring is off, you call a doctor up here right away."

The nurse would not call a doctor to my room. Lisa called her doctor who was home asleep at four in the morning, Lisa's doctor called my surgeon and demanded he get to the hospital right away. It was about six a.m. when Lisa's doctor came into my room looking a little disheveled and concerned. She looked me over quickly and left the room, she had gone to make a phone call. I think may have gone to see if my surgeon was on his way, he must have been, because then she left. Shortly after the Lisa's doctor left, Mom, Dad and Taz arrived to bring me home. I could hear my sister talking to Lisa right outside my door as they entered, when my surgeon came rushing to my room, telling my family to please wait in the hallway. All of a sudden there were nurses all over my room, disconnecting wires and connecting different equipment, they were preparing to take me to ICU. My surgeon asked me how I was feeling, I said, "Not so good, I've felt better."

He then gave me an injection and asked me again how did I feel I said, "I'm feeling better,"

That's all I remember, before I was leaving here.

From this point on, I was watching from the ceiling area at the hospital, the staff was in a frenzy trying to revive me, but it wasn't working. I could see my family in the hallway, they were upset, hugging and crying. I realized I had past away at this point.

My Mom, Dad, wife and sister entered the room where my body laid, my body was still warm as they touched me, caressed me, and kissed me crying. The look on my face wasn't one of confusion or anger nor distress, it looked like I was sleeping.

I had told my Mother before my surgery, that if God took me I was ready because he had another job for me. My sister told me not to talk like that, because I wasn't going anywhere and leave her alone. I take it whether I was really ready to go or not God had something else in store for me. There were so many things I had wanted to do with my wife, we enjoyed each other so much, we had a lot in common, Lisa and I were great buddies and lovers. It was as if I could hear sweet voices calling my name, sweet familiar voices calling me from somewhere else, voices I hadn't heard in a long time.

My brother and sister had been buried, I had always wanted to be cremated and sprinkled at sea. The ocean was my favorite place; I loved everything about the beach.

I don't think at first I was willing to go to the voices that called my name, I wanted to hang around for a while, but knew it was time to leave earth and go home. I will say a few nights after my service, everything had quieted down, my wife and oldest son were setting in the den watching television and a serving spoon fell out of the dish drainer onto the floor. I believe to this day they both still think it was me in the kitchen letting them know I'm here, and they might be right about this.

My sister Taz said one time, Heaven might not be far, far away, it might be here with us now, but in another dimension so that we can't see it, but once in a while we can feel it. Like when you get the feeling a departed loved one is near or you might do something your grandparent did when they were alive, yet you were too young to remember them or what they did. Who knows she might be right in some way.

Afterward

The moral to this story;
Don't look at a book's cover and think you know the inside story, there are reasons why people are the way they are or do the things they do. Consider this and put yourself in their shoes before judging a book by its cover.
Every day you live each day may be different, some days good and some days not so good, but each and every day no matter what it's like remember It's A Part of Life.

About the Author

Currently resides in New Jersey.
I am an expressionist.